Hünefeld den 28 Sept 1996

TAGE ANDERSEN

Text:
Aase Holm

Photographs:
Lennard
Stuart McIntyre
Rigmor Mydtskov
and
Bent Rej

BORGEN

TAGE ANDERSEN
© Borgens Forlag 1991
Cover and arrangement: Tage Andersen
Photo on front: Lennard
Photo on back: Lennard, Bent Rej and Stuart McIntyre
Reproduction: Carlsen
Printed by Kerteminde Tryk
Bookbinding: Nordisk Bogproduktion
Published by Borgens Forlag,
Valbygaardsvej 33, DK-2500 Copenhagen Valby

ISBN 87-418-6089-6 bound

First edition, 3rd printing, 1995

Photographs:

BENT REJ: pages 101, 118-119, 120-121, 122, 142 bottom right, 147, 148-149, 150, 165 left, 169, 170-171, 172-173, 174-175, 176-177, 178-179, 180-181, 182-183, 184-185, 186-187, 188-189, 190 bottom, 191, 192-193, 194, 195, 196-197, 202-203, 204-205, 206-207, 209, 210-211, 212-213, 215, 216, 217, 218-219, 220-221, 222-223, 224-225, 226-227, 228-229, 230, 232-233, 234-235, 236-237, 238-239

STUART MCINTYRE: pages 5, 12-13, 17 bottom, 32 top, 34 bottom, 69, 100, 114-115, 117, 119, 123, 124-125, 126, 127, 128-129, 130-131, 132-133, 136-137, 138-139, 140-141, 142 top, 145, 154 bottom, 155 top, 156, 158-159, 160-161, 162-163, 164, 190 top

LENNARD: pages 17 top, 24 top, 27, 28, 32 bottom, 33, 34 top, 39, 40-41, 42-43, 44-45, 49, 50-51, 52-53, 54-55, 56-57, 58-59, 61-62, 67, 68, 71, 72-73, 74 bottom, 75, 76-77, 78-79, 80-81, 82-83, 84-85, 86-87, 88-89, 90-91, 92, 93, 98-99, 102-103, 116, 120 left, 134-135, 142 bottom left, 143, 151, 152-153, 154 top, 155 bottom, 157, 165 right, 166-167, 168, 201, 231

RIGMOR MYDTSKOV: pages 1, 11, 14, 198-199, 200
PRESSEFOTO: pages 9, 24 bottom, 74 top, 110, 144
OLE WINTHER: page 29
OLE BJØRCK: pages 30, 31
VAGN-EBBE KIER: pages 46-47, 48
DORTE KROGH: pages 111, 112-113
JACOB MYDTSKOV: page 146

Thanks

This book is the realization of a dream, a project that has only been made possible through the fantastic enthusiasm and great support from a circle of professionals and close friends.

I would first like to thank Aase Holm the author and Vibeke Gad for inspiration and drive. Ant thank you to Peter Wibroe for friendly assistance. Thanks to my co-workers in the business with a special thank you to Jøk Wolckmann for invaluable help in your daily work with the book. Thanks too to Peter Olesen and Erik Crillesen from Borgens Forlag and Jess Christensen from Carlsen Repro.
And last but not least thanks to the flock of photographers who have followed me through the last 15 years: Lennard, Stuart McIntyre, Rigmor Mydtskov and Bent Rej.

The Shop

Tage Andersen's wonderful world

As a flower artist, Tage Andersen is unique, an original creative talent, whose name has become known in many countries in only a few years. To step into his world is like coming into a universe animated by magic and fairy-tale. From the first instant, the soul and the senses are enchanted in his fascinating world of flowers and are whirled into a torrent of experiences of great and mysterious beauty.

Tage Andersen's universe includes not only flowers in the ordinary sense but everything that grows. Strange growths from the abundance of the earth and the sea, from the exaggeratedly refined to the most humble. His scenarios are eccentric and luxurious, filled with drama and theatrical elements – an artist who works with life and death, with light and shade, in an eternal interplay between the extreme points of existence, often with an enchanting touch of decadence.

Tage Andersen creates his compositions with equal parts of art and craft. He is able to create things never seen before. His compositions are unpredictable and profoundly original.

It is the world of the baroque, in all its magnificence and contrastful expressiveness, that Tage Andersen opens up for the viewer and at his exhibitions at home and abroad in recent years his particular style has evoked admiration and recognition on a level with other expressions of art.

»As an artist, who tells his stories with flowers and plants, he is a great and original creator,« goes one quotation from international review.

Amongst buildings from the 1700s

Tage Andersen's shop, to which he moved in 1987 after a decade in the business on Kongens Nytorv, lies in Ny Adelgade, one of the oldest streets in Copenhagen, with buildings from the 1700s, and only a stone's throw from Kongens Nytorv, the city's distinguished square.

To call it a shop is an understatement. For behind the blue-black facade with tall flower-pillars, one is drawn into a space, where gravity appears to be abolished. A stone staircase leads down into the depths of the space and from there the shop spreads out on various levels.

The walls around the exciting sequences of spaces are painted in colours inspired by the reflections of the sky and the ocean, in blue-grey and blue-violet nuances, on which can be faintly discerned mysterious and living formations, which are, very prosaically, small organic spots of damp that Tage Andersen has allowed to remain on the raw walls and which he has worked up further into independent decorative elements.

And overhead float small white clouds, painted directly on to the ceiling.

Andersen's scenario tunes the mind in a quite special way. The senses are sharpened and the voice is muted in order to hear more distinctly the poetic sounds which fill his world; birds which warble and sing, water which murmurs.

It is not possible to perceive the whole of his image-rich world at one glance. Step by step, new experiences open up. Tage Andersen's flower compositions float on tall, slim, iron pedestals, are placed on impressive pillars, are built up of large, cubist steel boxes, or presented in exciting vases and baskets of glass and metal.

Tall and narrow mirrors with inset fields of matt-ground blue glass reflect the scenery grouped around the unique furniture he creates of iron and zinc; tables, pedestals and cupboards, benches for two or more, majestic high-backed chairs with large, blue precious stones for decoration or topped with a golden crown.

From the ceilings hang his uniquely artistic chandeliers, created of iron and decorated with the fruits of the sea and the earth, with sparkling play of light when the candles are reflected in cut-glass crystals. The chandeliers have the same variability as Tage Andersen's other compositions and are created to match the changing rhythms of the seasons – with great luxurious riches for Christmas festivities, sumptuous when the ripe fruit is harvested in the autumn, simple and poetic when the first signs of spring shoot forth.

The tranquillity and perspective of the balcony

With his unique flair for proportioning a space, in his shop Tage Andersen has created exciting leaps of level which define many spaces within the space, thus making the experience all the more manifold. Each of these spaces has its own atmosphere and offers its special experience in order to play symphonically together in the larger, superior perspective.

From one of the levels, a spiral staircase leads up to a balcony, which as a hanging garden entices investigation. With a virtuosic sweep, something new and astonishing, which raises and expands its dimensions completely, is added to the space's given limits.

If the floor level of the shop serves as the place for the daily bustle and communication (here the fresh flowers are placed in vases, here the customer and the assistant meet), then the balcony is place of almost meditative tranquillity.

Here Tage Andersen introduces his settings, as experiments, as games or directly as theatre and imaginative arrangements. One week the scene is set for a sensuous supper for two with porcelain, flower decorations, noble glass and zinc cutlery to his own design. The following week, new furniture models and objects will be shown in an astonishing and unusual layout.

There is a permanent exhibition of Tage Andersen's great creativity within the arrangement of the space.

The balcony has a different role in the great settings. From up here all the magnificence can be contemplated from the same angle and with the same feeling of weightlessness that a bird must have.

Flute concerto for exotic birds

Through the scenery sound charming calls from exotic and colourful birds in sumptuous cages and aviaries. Birds have a big place in Tage Andersen's world;

»They help to give the life and luxuriance that I like. Their song and movements give life to the building.«

And truly, the birds could hardly live more beautifully than in the Andersenian world. Tage Andersen has created the cages and aviaries with spaciousness and fantasy and they are filled every day with plants and fresh fruit. The birds have about them all the attention and communication that release a natural joy of song.

A completely special dialogue goes on between Tage Andersen and each individual bird. A couple of words, a chat is answered by a whole little flute concerto. A little close contact, perhaps a friendly nip of a finger or a pat on the bird's head, can become the overture to a true orchestral work, as all the birds, from one cage to another, outside and inside, tune in with all their glory of song.

The large, colourful Turako is a clear soloist in the choir, baying like a hound, with deep notes bringing associations with green jungles. Around it are other exotic representatives of the bird world, all just as fascinating, from the refined Chinese sunbird and Jacobsen the parrot to small busy quails.

The courtyard oasis with cascades of water

The fairy-tale world continues. From the balcony, the way leads past a little fountain out into the courtyard garden, to a fascinating new world laid out between beautiful old buildings from the 1700s.

In the centre of this oasis, quietly secluded from the sounds of the street, lies a large and elaborate glass-house with tower and spire. Beneath the glass cupola, a fountain sends its cascades of water down over floating water-lilies, whilst on high birds preen their feathers.

Beneath the open sky, the courtyard is laid with hand-hewn cobbles in patterns. Each morning, the stones are watered so that they are always bright and shining. Trees and plants which can defy the Northern climate grow here all the year round and when the mild winds announce themselves Tage Andersen moves his twisted bay trees and scented orange bushes out under the vault of the sky. They are placed amongst decorative constructions of iron and large granite pillars, which are the courtyard's fixed elements in an everchanging staging. In early summer, they have the company of café and garden furniture to Tage Andersen's own design, light chairs and tables in green-painted metal, and le Corbusier's wooden garden furniture with new Andersenian ideas added. A place of rest for eye and body.

A glance up and down the walls surrounding the courtyard and yet another wonderful sight presents itself, a vertically growing garden. Tage Andersen has his workshops, his studio and his living quarters in the building on the long side of the courtyard. On each of the stories, he has placed tall iron constructions and transformed them into hanging gardens, where bushes, flowers and trees grow. The uppermost of these semi-circular projections, closest to the sun and the blue sky, is equipped as a giant aviary.

The Artist

The vault of heaven and nature as inspiration

Tage Andersen was born in north-west Denmark, in the area of Thy, where sky and earth are marked by the neighbourhood of the great ocean. The horizon is wide, the sky endless but in winter-time the storm brings bush and tree to their knees.

There were no factors, either in his childhood home or the environment, which pointed directly towards an artistic path for the youngest one of the family's two sons. However, a few of his early recollections could well have given a hint.

As a child in the country, Tage Andersen, who was born in 1947, was to a large extent, left to the form of play which his own imagination could devise. And he remembers, how he, even before he began school, made figures from the branches and things he found in nature. He became completely absorbed by the creative, when he had a teacher in school who allowed the pupils to set up historical scenes to sharpen their interest in their reading. There Tage Andersen threw himself with glowing eagerness into total theatre and made figures and scenery for the performances of the doll's theatre, creating imaginative costumes from the materials to hand for all the historical gallery.

After seven years at school, at the age of fourteen, he wanted to be either a forester, a vet or a gardener.

It was to be the latter possibility and he was apprenticed to a local nursery. However, working with plants in their tender beginnings swiftly showed itself to fit in badly with his enquiring and creative mind. He felt that it took too long before the seeds and seedlings grew into the plants and flowers he would rather be occupied with. He therefore swapped the black earth for cake dough and marzipan and was trained as a confectioner in a fine, old, provincial confectioner's and bakery.

The first shop and fame

When he was twenty, he opened his first shop with flowers and fruit. After a number of years in this home-town, he looked for larger horizons, first educating himself further as a confectioner at the distinguished, old Conditori Emmery in Aarhus, before some years later opening a new and larger shop with the flower art that has since created his fame. It was in the period around this shop in Viborg, that attention was directed in earnest at Tage Andersen.

He was discovered by the press and both his flower art and his arrangements became the object of long articles in magazines and weeklies. Orders came from all over the country and amongst the many who approached him was the Copenhagen flowerseller with a Royal Warrant, Svend Schaumann, who invited Tage Andersen to come to Copenhagen and use his special talents in constructing spectacular large flower arrangements for the Royal Family and for official occasions.

For a number of years, Tage Andersen's activities took place partly in his business in Viborg and partly in connection with the big projects in Copenhagen. The collaboration with Schaumann led in 1976 to Tage Andersen taking over Schaumann's famous shop on Kongens Nytorv in Copenhagen.

It was also in this period that Tage Andersen presented the Copenhageners with a concept they had never seen before, a Flower Confectioner's, which he set up on one floor in the middle of the main pedestrian street. Here he combined his two great talents and invited the public into an exceptional visual world, where the confectioner's art and flower art were practised side by side. The guests drank coffee and ate Tage Andersen's small masterpieces of cakes whilst he himself created the bouquets and compositions they had ordered. The Flower Confectioner's on Vimmelskaftet lasted, however, only a short time, for the new shop on Kongens Nytorv demanded all his energies.

The child's respect for the great

The place where one is born and grows up marks one's attitude to nature throughout life. In Tage Andersen's case, the childhood countryside in the imposing and often harsh, Jutland landscape has brought affection and respect for the great and original.

In no other place does the sky seem so infinitely high as in this landscape between sea and loch, and in no other place are the rhythm of the sea and the colours of the landscape experienced more strongly. From his early childhood, Tage Andersen's favourite colours have been the blue nuances of sky and sea, his preferred month September with its great vault of heaven.

To a greater degree than the townsman, he who grows up in the countryside is at once observant of and dependant upon the weather and its changes and has to relate to them. For Tage Andersen, this ballast from a childhood lived on the land means that, in the midst of urban life, he also follows and senses the changes in the weather and the passing of the seasons:

»I love the northern winter months when the cold freezes earth and trees fast in graphic images. Some people perceive winter as sombre and poor but I feel that it is one of the most beautiful times of the year because it gives us the possibility of observing every little plant and each single tree and its special form.«

Tage Andersen experiences the same thrill in nature in spring, when an apple tree stands there with its thousands of white blossoms, an abundance of gifts and yet so simple. When the same tree later swells with its fruit, he experiences a great outpouring of joy at the munificence of nature.

»But autumn, which is the culmination, the climax of all that grows, is the most fantastically sumptuous. The landscape is never more dramatic than when everything is exploding in colour and in my shop this is a time so full of excitement and delight.«

Human warmth

Tage Andersen's life in covenant with nature has also left its traces on his character and personality. He is a harmonious person with his feet on the ground. His gaze is steady, his body language full of strength, always clad in plus-fours and a shirt of soft material in subdued colours, his hair gathered in knot on his nape, a silk sharf tied about his neck. A pair of warm, inquisitive eyes peer from behind the gold-rimmed glasses under a broad-brimmed hat. Tage Andersen in his physiognomy resembles a Renascence man.

He willingly acknowledges his need for sumptuousness:
»The sumptuous can also be created from simple things and I love beauty and cannot exist without creating. I have a great passion for nature, flowers and animals and my life, as I live it today, is the fulfilment of my dreams. I am surrounded by the things I work with and care about in an atmosphere of interdependence. Regardless of where I find myself in my building, I am close to these things. They are my life, my world.«

If one asks him where his rich flood of ideas comes from, he answers:
»It comes from within.«

The Flowers

Each day brings its wonders

Tage Andersen begins his working day before night becomes day. He starts the car between five and six in the morning and drives out to market, where his suppliers are ready to present their specialities from the world of flowers.

With the vehicle packed to breaking point, he drives through the dawning day back to town, stopping on the way at Frederiksberg Gardens to go for a brisk walk through the park, to say good-night to the moon and good-morning to the new day. His two dachshunds make the morning walk into a lively occasion with fixed rituals amongst the twittering birds in the park's trees, the cackling ducks on the canals and the scampering squirrels.

Back home in the shop, his co-workers await with great expectations for what Tage Andersen will bring back from the morning's expedition. Is it one of those days, where the very first examples of a wonderful kind of flower are to fill the atmosphere of the shop? With which new flowers, which fruits, which colours will they be working today? All of this is of great significance for how the day is to be planned and will go.

The following hours are proof that flower art is borne upon talent but that the touch of the craftsman has just as great a significance. The workshops behind the shop are transformed into a living world of flowers where people work with concentration and verve.

Every single one of the hundreds of fresh flowers is taken up, stalk by stalk, cleared of foliage, not too little, not too much, and freshly cut before being placed in cold water. The flowers are handled with great care and are treated as the living organisms which they are:

»Be careful. Do not shake the flowers and take care not to knock their heads,« says the omnipresent Tage Andersen.

He himself is doing wonderful things, pinching and plucking with a sure hand so that ordinary flowers are in his hands transformed to surprising new plants.

Just as the author Karen Blixen did in her bouquets at Rungstedlund, Tage Andersen removes many of the green leaves from the flowers.

»It is too ordinary with all that greenery. It dominates and destroys the experience of the flower's special form and colour. It is the sculptural form of the flower that interests me. This gives the signals and messages I want to bring out.«

The shop reflects the rhythm of nature

What is singular about Tage Andersen's business is that it always follows and mirrors the rhythm of the year. Nature lives on within his walls.

The day the violets blossom, Tage Andersen fills the shop with their scent and poetry. That day, they stand in simple little pots or scented bouquets as the principal actors, giving notice that now spring has come.

When the scented woodruff breaks through the black earth and is collected by people who know where it grows, he ties them in wreaths and bouquets and the whole room is filled with their spicy scent.

The blue grape hyacinths, fragile and shy in stature, become like the fanfare for spring itself, when he packs hundreds tightly together as a carpet of dusty blue.

The first tulips are celebrated with sumptuous bouquets of the rarest and loveliest kinds of this harbinger of spring. And when the calender reaches May, Tage Andersen brings the first beautiful lilies-of-the-valley.

»Today, there are many people who have lost the feeling for the seasons and the changing gifts of nature. I can often demonstrate that there are people who do not know when the various kinds of flower blossom and have their true season at all and I feel that this is a sad symbol of civilization,« says Tage Andersen.

High summer, festivities and joy of life, that is when the roses come. In extravagant displays, not ten but a hundred of the finest sorts are presented, in cascades like an oriental fairy-tale.

Autumn, the deep shades of colour, dahlias with blood-red blooms. The first turgid, dewy grapes. Imposing thistles in waxy blue shades. Wonderful fruits from foreign shores and Danish cabbages in mysterious power and splendour.

Winter, the soft moss crawling with life, the crooked branch formations of fairy-tale, mistletoe and holly, the first hellebors. And a New Year, lilacs forced under glass, with intoxicating scent from their fragile flower clusters.

Each bouquet is created individually

A Tage Andersen bouquet never resembles anything anyone has seen before. You do not go to his shop to buy ten tulips tied together with string. Each bouquet is created individually, sculpturally, with surprising, often shocking constellations.

Tage Andersen questions those who ask him to make a bouquet. What is the bouquet to celebrate or mark? Is the recipient a girl, a boy, woman or man and of what temperament? Bouquets are very personal things, flowers give signals, they are symbols. Tage Andersen listens and makes his bouquet.

With a sure hand he builds up his composition. Here there is no hesitation and no room for regret either, for the bouquet has its own life right from the beginning.

The bridal bouquet, the most romantic of them all, the one giving memories for a lifetime, is a special discipline. The procedure starts with an introduction to the prospective bride and a conversation about the arrangements for the wedding solemnities themselves. If it is a matter of a big church wedding, then the details of the wedding dress, the material, the style, are all gone through. If the bride is to wear a veil, how will the hair be set?

Tage Andersen will work for many hours to achieve the perfect result, where every single blossom is put on thread so that it can be built into the sculptural form of the bridal bouquet, and he often accompanies the bride to the porch to give the final touches.

»Do women today still save their bridal bouquets?«

»Yes, of course, and, as always in the world of romance, it is the most beautiful thing to let the bouquet die upon the dressing table and dry naturally,« answers Tage Andersen.

Dramatic and fascinating forms

To see Tage Andersen's compositions come into being is like opening the door to a fascinating new world. In contrast to the bouquets, the dried compositions have a long development. Tage Andersen often works for several weeks before he has brought out the expression he wants. Some flowers have to be completely fresh when they are used, others should be so far advanced in the process that they have the beauty of decay. He adds something to the composition each day, it matures on the way.

Plants too are an area of fascination in Tage Andersen's realm. Through him, long forgotten plants have been given a renascence and can be seen again in the glass pavilion and the green courtyard. The sharp Mother-Law's Tongue, the dramatic Agave or, for example, Muehlenbeckia with its tiny leaves. A special place in his world has the evergreen Ivy, which has been the object of creative experiments with forms and figures and which is also in his logo.

When he opened his shop on Kongens Nytorv, he presented for the first time his special ivy-art with a whole landscape of ivy-trees shaped into classic figures such as spheres, squares and obelisks. They soon turned out to be born classics and immediately became the fashion.

Tage Andersen has since developed the possibilities of the luxuriant ivy to the full. One well-known example is his botanical chair, quite overgrown with green ivy. Another composition is a graceful octagonal pavilion wreathed in ivy. This was inspired by a popular tourist attraction at one of the royal castles in Copenhagen, namely, the pavilion on the little bridge leading to the Chinese teahouse that the Danish King Frederik VI built by Frederiksberg Castle.

The change of seasons and the festivals also inspire him to imaginative variations, in springtime, a bird's nest built of ivy, for Easter, large ivy cockerels proudly waving their tail-feathers.

Just like Karen Blixen, who also was a passionate floral creator, Tage Andersen too has a feeling for cabbages. The sculptural form and dark Renascence colours of the brassicas inspired them both and they are often included in Tage Andersen's settings, from the curly leaves of kale at Christmas to the tender shoots of red cabbage in serried ranks in the spring.

Would it be possible for a man like Tage Andersen to name just one flower as his preference if he had to make a choice?

Would it be the simple blue Gentian, which he uses so poetically and imaginatively in all the summer compositions?

Or the almost divine Camellia, so delicate and fine that it keeps it scent to itself, so imposing that everything else pales beside it . . .?

The Settings

Interior and furniture in total pictures

As an interior designer, Tage Andersen, in his shop, in his arrangements and at his exhibitions, creates the total pictures which are his ideal.

»Everything has to be co-ordinated, materials, proportions and colours, to achieve the atmosphere and totality I want. The flowers are the starting point, but they are not enough in themselves to express the special mood I wish to achieve,« he says.

The design of furniture, lighting, glass, vases, flower-pots, baskets, tableware, textiles — the objects for the space as a whole — are also part of his many activities. He frequents the workshop environment with the same professional self-assurance as the world of flowers. Those hands, which sensitively shape bouquets, become big, strong paws at the smith's, the potter's and the glass-blower's.

From the potter, Tage Andersen gets his pitchers and pots with rich decorations of grapes, conch shells and doves or dramatic lion's heads. From the candlemaker, he has his lovely patinated candles in coloured stearin. From Florence come his sophisticated silk ribbons. And his glass goblets, vases and drinking glasses with the conch shell for inspiration, are created in collaboration with the glass artist Darryle Hinz.

An award in the Guide Michelin

His furniture is unique, spectacular; created in iron, with traces of the craftsman's tools as a decorative element of the expression. From this hard, almost brutal material, he shapes his collection, which includes tables, cupboards, sofas, benches and chairs of many kinds.

The language is that of the baroque and every single piece of furniture carries Tage Andersen's seal. Some of the pieces, produced in limited editions, are numbered and signed. Others were originally created for a particular interior, for example, the high-backed dining chairs that form part of Tage Andersen's design of Restaurant Kommandanten in Copenhagen, and have now gone into wider production.

Another Copenhagen restaurant equipped by Tage Andersen is Restaurant Nouvelle. Here the tableware he created in zinc is used and Nouvelle is the only restaurant in Denmark to be given an award in the *Guide Michelin* for its tasteful decor.

The crazy is the spice of existence

Tage Andersen satisfies his need for big settings on the stage, at the circus or in church, different as they are.

His debut was as early as 1970, when he was given a big project in Copenhagen Cathedral, and TV teams from several countries came.

Tage Andersen organized the large foyer of the church around an exhibition of icons painted by a good inspiratory friend, Peter Egor, the now deceased Danish icon-painter, and shown in the cathedral in connection with the World Ecumenical Year. One reviewer wrote that »Tage Andersen has transformed a normally dismal space into Aladdin's fairy palace.«

In the autumn of 1990, Tage Andersen was the stage designer for the performance at the New Theatre about Herman Bang's *Intermission* with Erik Mørk of the Royal Theatre in the only role. The performance took place in the stuccoed ballet hall of the theatre and Tage Andersen created not only the scenery, costumes and furniture but drew the whole of the theatre into his setting. The seats for the public were reupholstered and before each performance scented rose geraniums were strewn between the rows. There were real, scented flowers on the stage. The birds in the cage were not artificial but canaries full of life.

The producer Flemming Behrendt wrote of Tage Andersen's design for the big chaise longue in the performance that »it was so big that it seemed to burst the bounds of the fragile scenery. But then we discovered what it was that Tage wanted; to extend the inner world of Bang into a large theatrical symbol which the Freudians might call a womb.«

The circus has a big place in Tage Andersen's heart. He will travel far to experience it. For premieres of the Danish Circus Benneweis, he has made almost ecstatic decorations and he himself says of the inspiration that the travelling circus world has given him:

»I am fascinated by how often they are successful in creating a festival performance in often extremely primitive conditions. Each day, from town to town, hard work and hard training has to shine in a new and perfect performance.«

Tage Andersen is not a man of the conventions, the straight lines. He wants a life of beauty. The crazy is the spice of existence.

The big exhibitions

Brandt's Pakhus
Tage Andersen opened his first one-man show in 1985. This happened in Brandt's Pakhus in Copenhagen and there the public met a flower-artist (with the emphasis on artist) par excellence.

With his large compositions and baroque arrangements in which he combined different things, porcelain, iron and live materials, Tage Andersen appealed to a new artistic attitude and the exhibition was crucial to his career.

Many of the exhibition's objects had surrealistic overtones and on the poster he presented a composition in which several of his well-known symbols were gathered. Under the branches of the camellia tree, a snail bears violets, a dove sits on a pumpkin and a cabbage stands amongst brightly coloured blooms.

Bakkehuset
In 1985, in Bakkehus Museum in Frederiksberg held an exhibition called *Tage Andersen in Bakkehuset*. There, with magnificent large bouquets of garden flowers and with large compositions illustrating the epoch's culture, he blew fresh life into a well-preserved cultural environment of the early 1800s.

Charlottenborg
On the occasion of the ten years anniversary of his business in 1986, Tage Andersen held his hitherto largest exhibition of *Wondrous Trees* at Charlottenborg. This was the first time an exhibition had been held in the palace courtyard and, for the presentation of his trees, Tage Andersen erected half-a-dozen glass pavilions in the symmetrical layout, the special blue light of which had always fascinated him.

In her review of the exhibition in *Politiken*, Libbie Fjeldstrup wrote:
»These are really quite wonderful, strange and incredible trees, which Tage has thought of here. None of them, be they large or small, can be found in any garden, unless it be Paradise. All around in many-sided glass pavilions, this baroque flower artist, as original in mind as in appearance, has placed more than fifty imaginative experiences, most of them indescribable, as words are insufficient to explain the mixture of fairy-tale, humour, romance, reverie and fantasy that Tage Andersen has constructed with his tanned flower hands. Everything one sees, does not exist in reality. Who has ever seen a tree of mussels? An obelisk of magnolia leaves? Or twisted branches with flowers of iron, sugar or marzipan? And so it goes on and on in Tage Andersen's wonderful

world, where that determined by nature is abolished and replaced with the strange beauties of the imagination.«

Throughout the opening day, where young waiters in artist's smocks served champagne and a flute trio played baroque music, Tage Andersen drove his guests in a horse-drawn charabanc across Kongens Nytorv from his shop on the other side of the square.

The exhibition at Charlottenborg brought Tage Andersen a prize from the Danish State Art Fund. At the same time, it marked the end of ten happy years on Kongens Nytorv, where his window exhibitions with their stream of changing pictures towards the world had taken on the character of a place of pilgrimage for visitors and inhabitants of the city alike.

Rosenborg Castle
In 1988, the year after the move to the new shop in Ny Adelgade, Tage Andersen exhibited at Rosenborg Castle on the occasion of the quatercentenary of the enthronment of Christian IV.

Together with the goldsmith Birte Stenbak, he was invited to do the decorations for a Royal banquet at the exhibition; an invitation and, at the same time, a wonderful opportunity to fly on the wings of fantasy. Tage Andersen set the banquet table, between the pawned Royal silver loaned for the occasion by the Kremlin, with show dishes as he imagined them from the time of Christian IV.

As a tribute to the monarch's interest in animals, he created his compositions so that the abundance of desserts was proffered by animals. Magnificent arrangements of fruit were borne by elephants. A two-metre high portal with silver-plated apples was carried on the backs of Chinese dogs. A surrealistic promegranate tree in a glass pavilion (see the book's cover) was conveyed by horses, whilst magnificent lions balanced between great globes created of ivy-leaves.

The Orangery
In 1988, Tage Andersen packed a convoy of lorries and crossed with his whole ménage to England for his first one-man exhibition abroad.

The magnificent Orangery in Holland Park was placed at his disposal and there he held his hitherto largest exhibition with 85 large compositions and more than 300 units.

Thirty-six hours after the convoy's arrival, the exhibition was ready to accept London's festively dressed international public.

The show in London was Tage Andersen's first exhibition to include furniture and interior design and he filled the high-ceilinged space with his furniture, chandeliers and flower compositions, with pillars and tall mirrors between the ten metres high arched windows out to the park. He had also brought with him lighting specially created for the exhibition; a tree of light with a crown of small halogen lamps.

Tage Andersen brought with him to his London exhibition the life and movement that are so important in his world as well. A flock of wonderful birds were obtained, with the providential help of English bird fanciers, to dwell in his large fairy-tale birdcages throughout the exhibition.

The Ikon Exhibition
On the tenth day after the exhibition in London closed, Tage Andersen opened a Christmas exhibition in Copenhagen. A young Italian icon-painter, Mara Maccari, was the guest exhibitor in his shop, in a Byzantine atmosphere of incense and Gregorian chant. The private view a half-hour before midnight had the solemn atmosphere of a church.

Millesgård
From June to September in 1991, Tage Andersen will be holding his largest exhibition to date at Millesgården near Stockholm.

At Lidingö, where the sculptor Carl Milles had his high-lying studio in the magnificent skerry landscape, Tage Andersen will move in and fill the place with his special art. Inside and outside, in studios and on terraces, he will create a scenario which at once interacts with and is challenged by Milles' strong, almost awe-inspiring sculptures.

Dancers from the Royal Danish Ballet will emphasize the enchantment of the northern summer with their midsummer dance between the pillars.

North Jutland Art Museum
Two further exhibitions will contribute to making 1991 Tage Andersen's busiest year hitherto, namely an exhibition at the North Jutland Art Museum in Aalborg and a big exhibition in Germany in the autumn. 1991 is also the year in which Tage Andersen has gathered together the comprehensive pictorial material and created the graphic design for this book on his life and work.

Throughout the years, Tage Andersen has received many invitations to open businesses in the large cities of Europe: London, Hamburg, Düsseldorf, Milan and Florence. However, with his temperament and his perfectionist demands, he prefers to stay put in one place.

Even though he likes to travel, especially in Italy, whose landscapes, colours and intensity exercise a strong attraction over him, he has, like his favourite flowers, his roots in Denmark. He knows the landscapes and gardens of his fatherland, which he *has* to re-experience and which he cannot live without.

1977: one of my first windows on Kongens Nytorv.
At that time, I endeavoured to make my pictures out onto the world in a solemn, royal style.
Here mainly camellias and French roses are built up in pyramids.

Window on Kongens Nytorv in 1978 dedicated to Mother's Day, with the emphasis on roses. That year I launched dried roses for the first time. The white boxes contain dried bouquets of roses. The cornucopia that carries the blooms is covered with leaves.

Here lavender and various seed-heads. 1977-78 period.

Examples from the same period showing how we prepared and sold dry flowers.

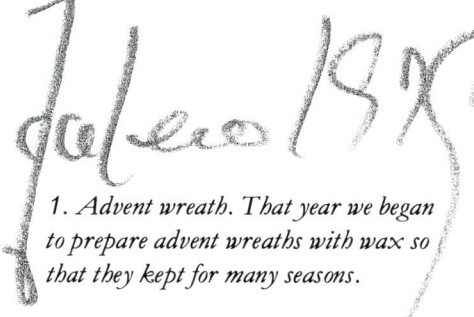

1. *Advent wreath. That year we began to prepare advent wreaths with wax so that they kept for many seasons.*

2. *Special project: giant Christmas wreath as table decoration for restaurateur Jan Hurtigkarl. In the centre, petits fours on a tray. There are dried roses in the cones made from leaves.*

3. *This Christmas tree in ivy is from 1978 and has since become a tradition.*

Cornucopias en masse from Christmas 1978. This was held very much in the confectioner's style. For example, we launched our marzipan fruits for the first time.

*At that time we held special week-end exhibitions, just as we made exhibitions for special occasions.
This one must have been Easter, as I have placed golden eggs in the green wreath.*

These cornucopias were the signs over the facade of my Flower Confectioner's on Strøget in Copenhagen.

I ran the place in conjunction with the shop on Kongens Nytorv. Many ideas were realized here but it ended as an enormous economic fiasco.

For a period, I had combined dwelling and studio in this courtyard house. From here I also ran a school in flower art, 1980-81.

This living curtain is Asparagus phalcatis, *which is standing only in water into the bargain.*

A collaboration with the fashion designer Jean Voigt in 1979 when we made a bridal show where he did the clothes and I did the flowers.
In the picture above can be seen Kirsten Ekkløw, Norway's foremost flower artist of the time, who assisted me with the show.

1980, when I am beginning to work more sculpturally and to include interiors in my world. To the right, a youthful me can be seen in front of the shop on Kongens Nytorv.

Above and below: creations with chairs, which always has been a preoccupation of mine. The »moulded« ivy-trees are created by tacking on the individual leaves.

Camellia blooms floating in water.

Dried and limed arum lilies.

The shape of an egg has always fascinated me; here, for the first time, as a sculpture in ivy leaves. One of spring's most well-known symbols here in the shop is probably the trees with bird's nests. They have become a tradition, although we have developed them through time.

Preserved eggs and sprouting potatoes. In the centre a single butterbur. Why not . . .?

Memories with fritillaria – snake's head fritillary and crown imperial.

Surrealistic composition under a glass bell.

Now we are in 1982, when I was asked by Interflora, Denmark, both to decorate their stand at the World Exhibition in Hamburg and represent Denmark in the world championship in flower decoration. On this page, pictures from the Danish stand. Miss Andersen, my faithful co-worker through the years, proudly presents The Little Mermaid, *which I regard as the most well-known symbol of Denmark, created from leaves laid like scales. The upper torso is a composition in every conceivable Danish garden flower.*

Here my interest in working with metals started, as you can see, from the chequered zinc floor.

The next page shows my bridal bouquet for the competition, displayed by Rita Pedersen, my assistant for the competition.

1982

One of the projects: a table setting. Porcelain and glass by the artist Arje Griegst.

The cutlery was specially designed and decorated by the goldsmith Birte Stenbak.

One of my pupils, Henrik Djernis, regarding one of his »master's« works.

Back home, they waited anxiously . . .
I did not become world champion.
But I can take credit for disturbing
many norms and for setting new tones.

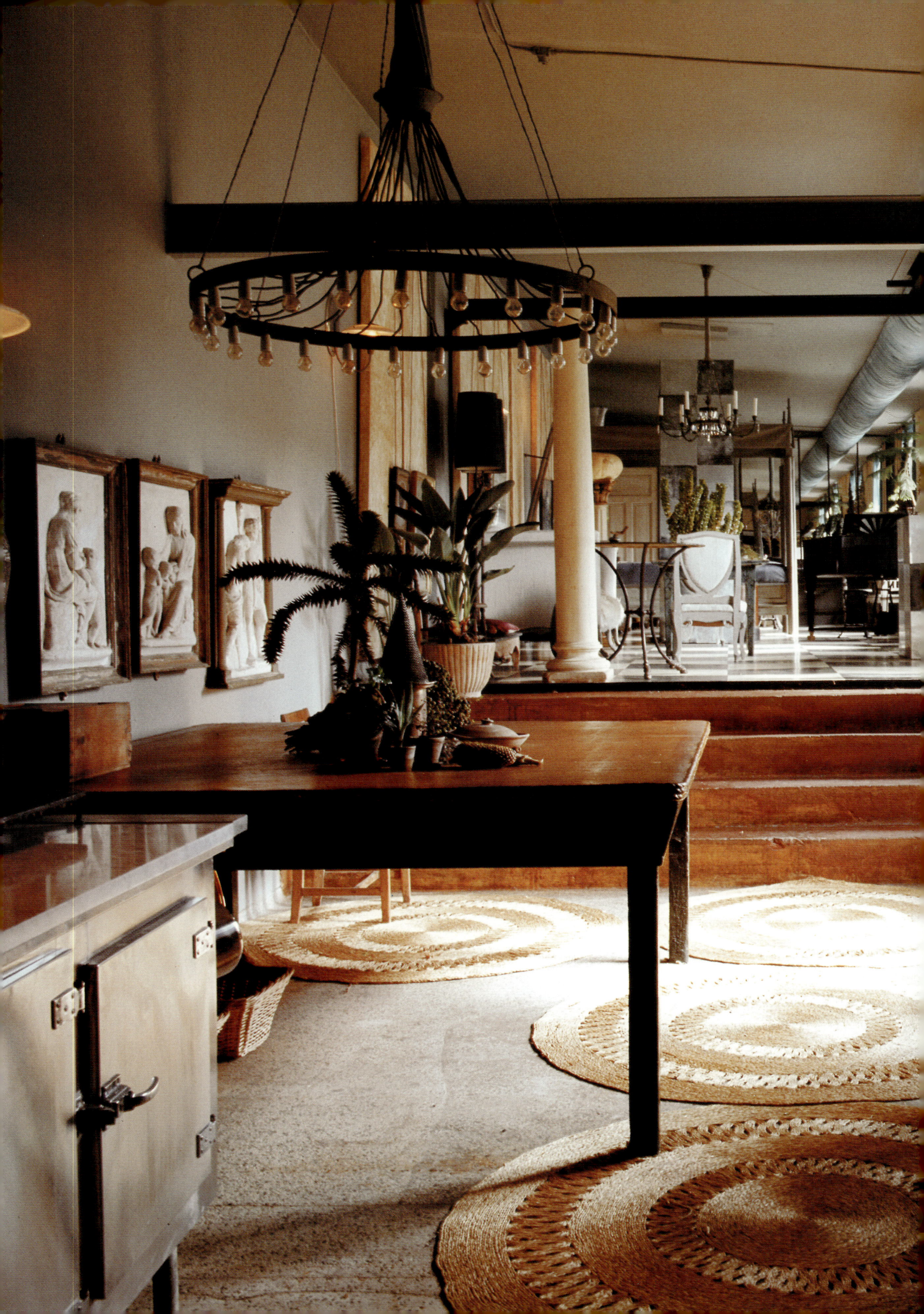

For a time, I loved moving and here I have set myself up in an old factory, which served partly as living accomodation and partly, for periods, as studio. The space had a rather interesting format of 5 × 23 metres.

Details from the accommodation on the previous page. Here there is an amusing interplay between the fern-fronds and the tired, draped curtains.

Strangely enough, the pumpkin with the dove has followed me throughout the years.

Imagine if there had been champagne in just one of the taps.

Pictures from a gigantic wedding decoration of Holmen's Church in Copenhagen.
Left: Part of a portal by the entrance.
Right: The bridal bouquet itself, which in all its simplicity consisted of auriculas surrounded by the well-known Tønder lace.

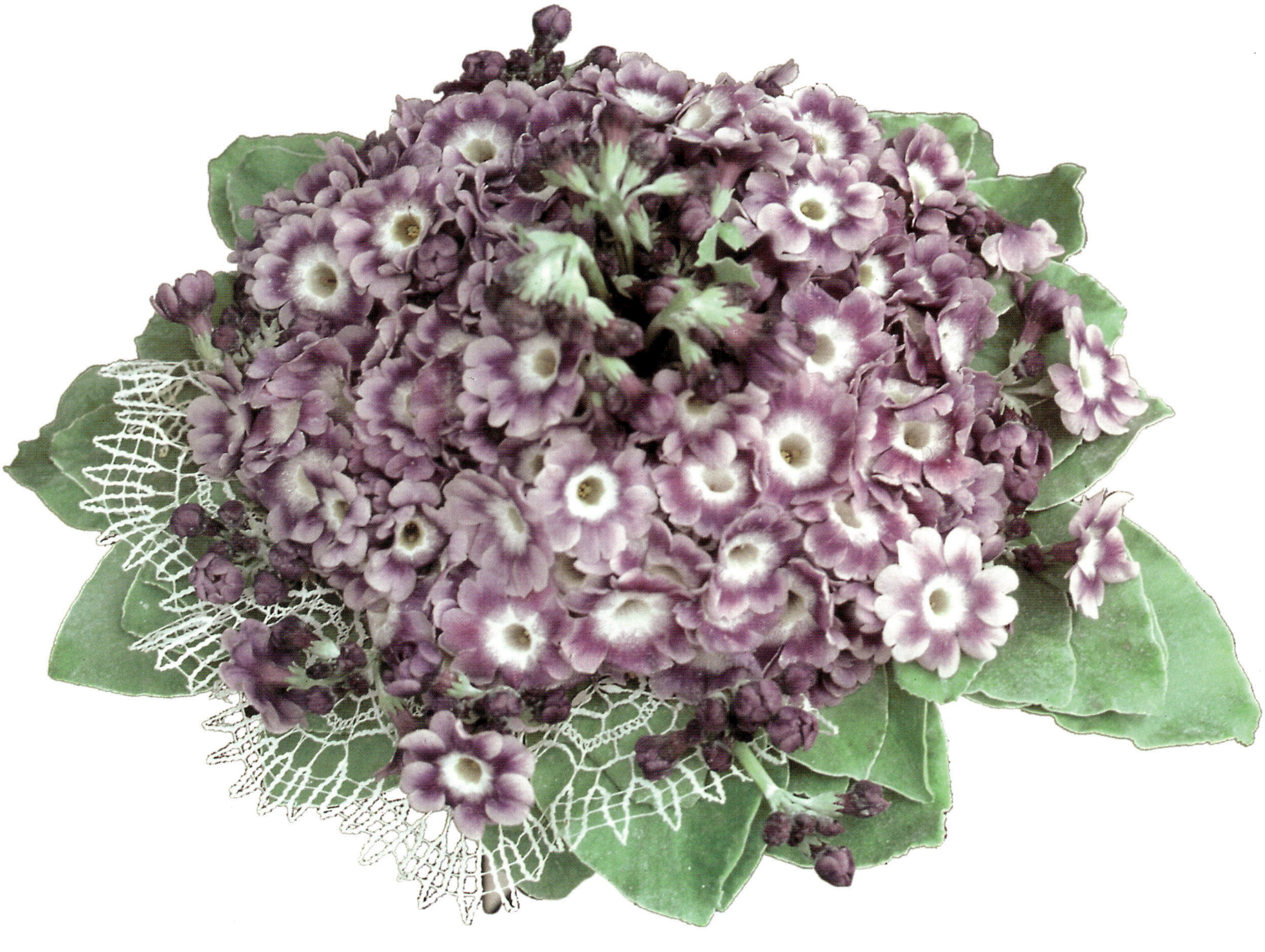

Tall pillars were places in the centre of the nave of the church. They were constructed of newly-opened beech leaves, bracken and maidenhair fern. The altar, which bore thousands of carnations, was flanked by camellia and buxus trees.

Late summer window, 1984, Kongens Nytorv. I believe that the chandeliers were the first of their kind I made.

Royal window on Kongens Nytorv on the occasion of the fiftieth birthday of His Royal Highness Prince Henrik.
The obelisk to the left was a commission, a gift to the Prince, and one of the first of my more monumental works in living plants.

On the next page: my window in honour of the Crown Prince's 18th. birthday. The crown at the top of the picture was taken from an exhibition at Rosenborg Castle and was made by Birte Stenbak from my idea.

Tromme er skabt af Kort Stedeli (Rosenborg Slot?)

A »baroque« arrangement. The flowers are mainly roses, respectively from nature, of paper and of plastic. From the exhibition of Brandt's Pakhus in 1985.

A game in forms and colours.

A bridal bouquet of a more dramatic and sculptural character.

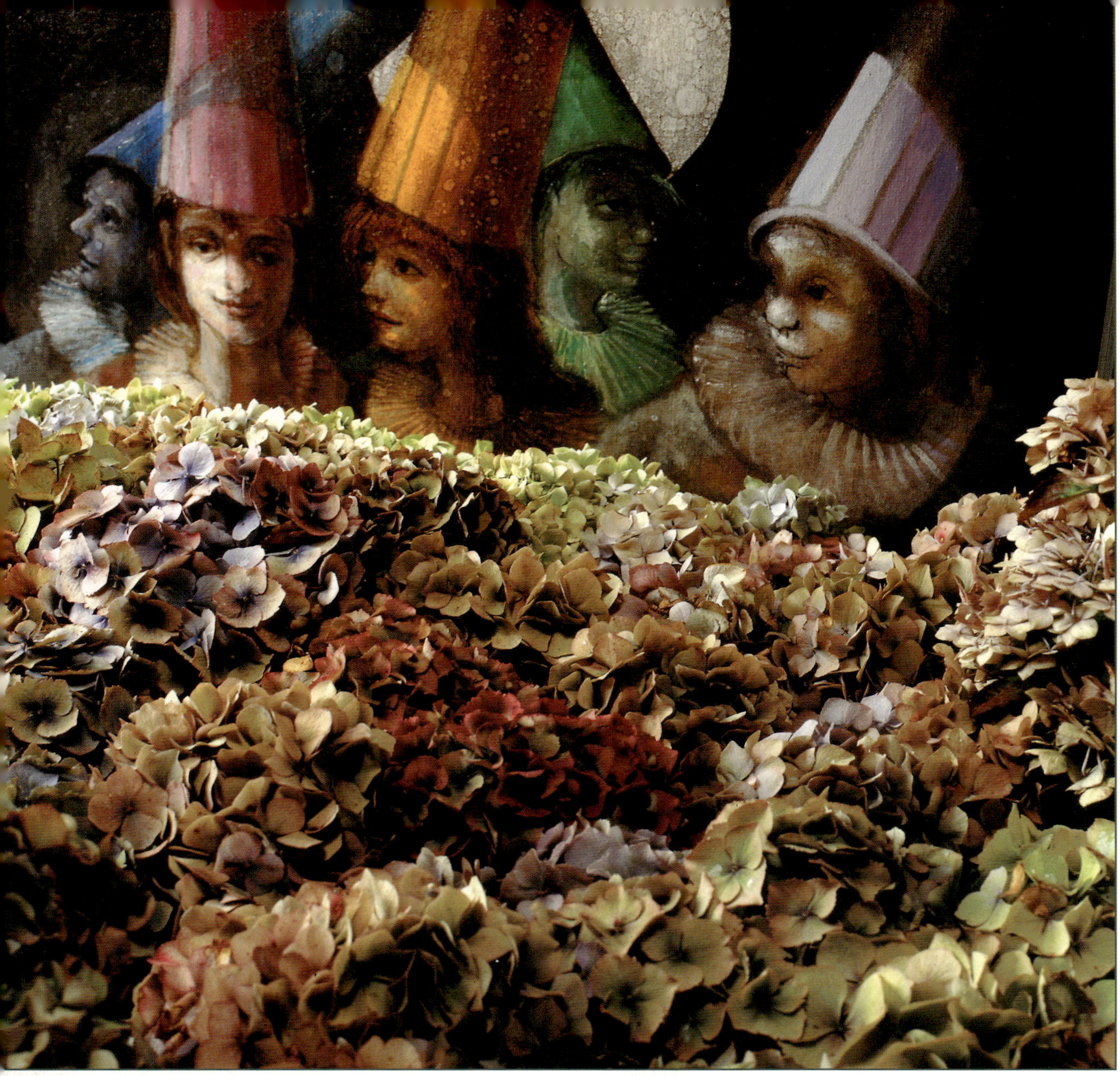

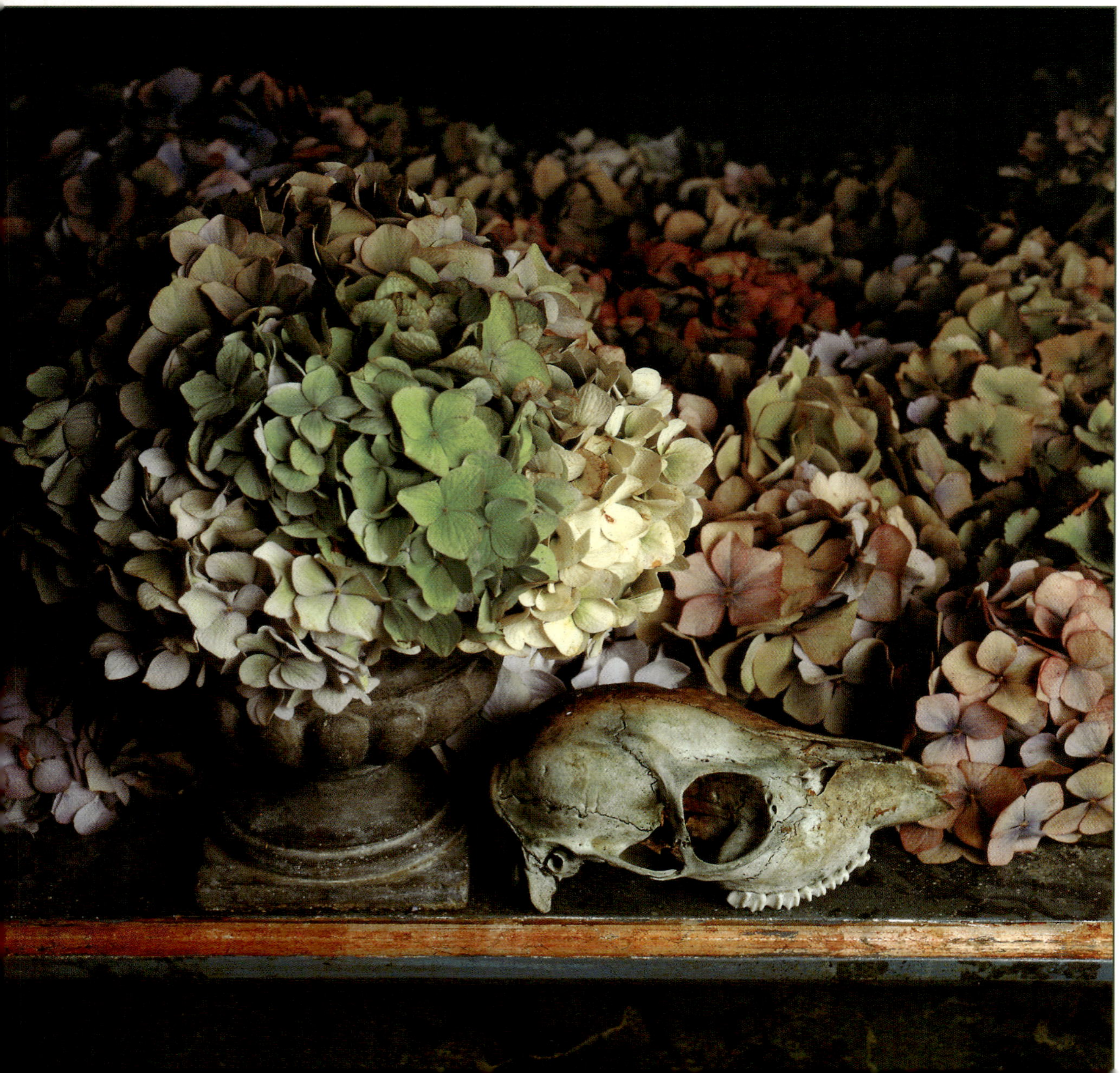

Is this perhaps a stage setting or has it all just been laid out to dry? Anything is possible...
Colour compositions with hydrangeas.

Dummy or reality?
The privet to the left is alive, as is the camellia with added real citrus fruits. The remaining trees are dummies, with marzipan fruit. The dummy trees were created to decorate a restaurant.

The composition was created as a centre-piece for my Christmas window in 1984 and later »appeared« at Restaurant Kong Hans. It was then divided up and the different levels took on their own separate existence.

Interior from the shop on Kongens Nytorv. At this time, the walls were partially covered with old French murals. I am partial to this form of exhibition as it also serves as an inspiration for my work and, at the same time, gives the space the air of a gallery or museum more than of a true shop. Notice here, for the first time, the chequered floors, which were originally inspired by the floors in Liselund Museum.

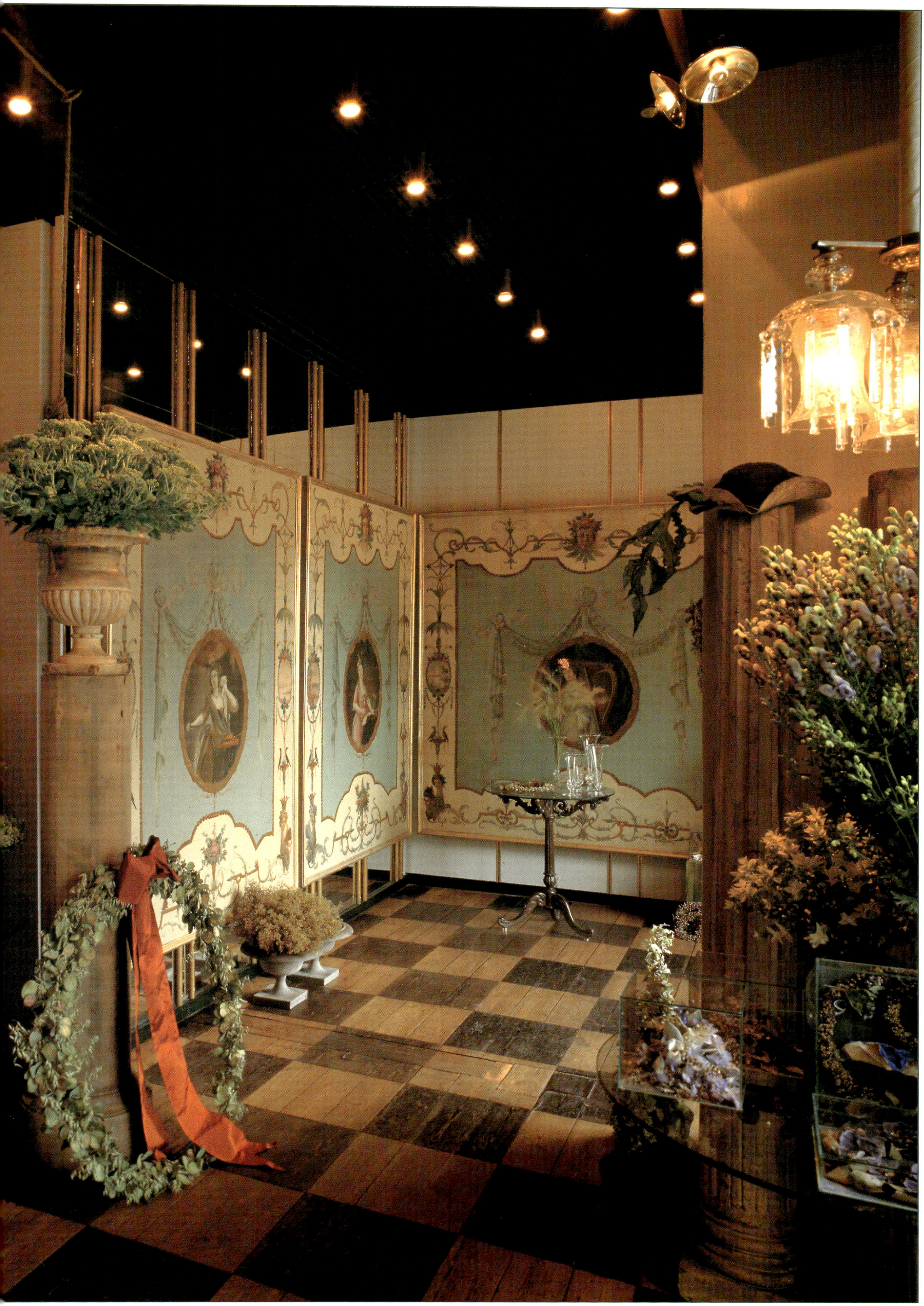

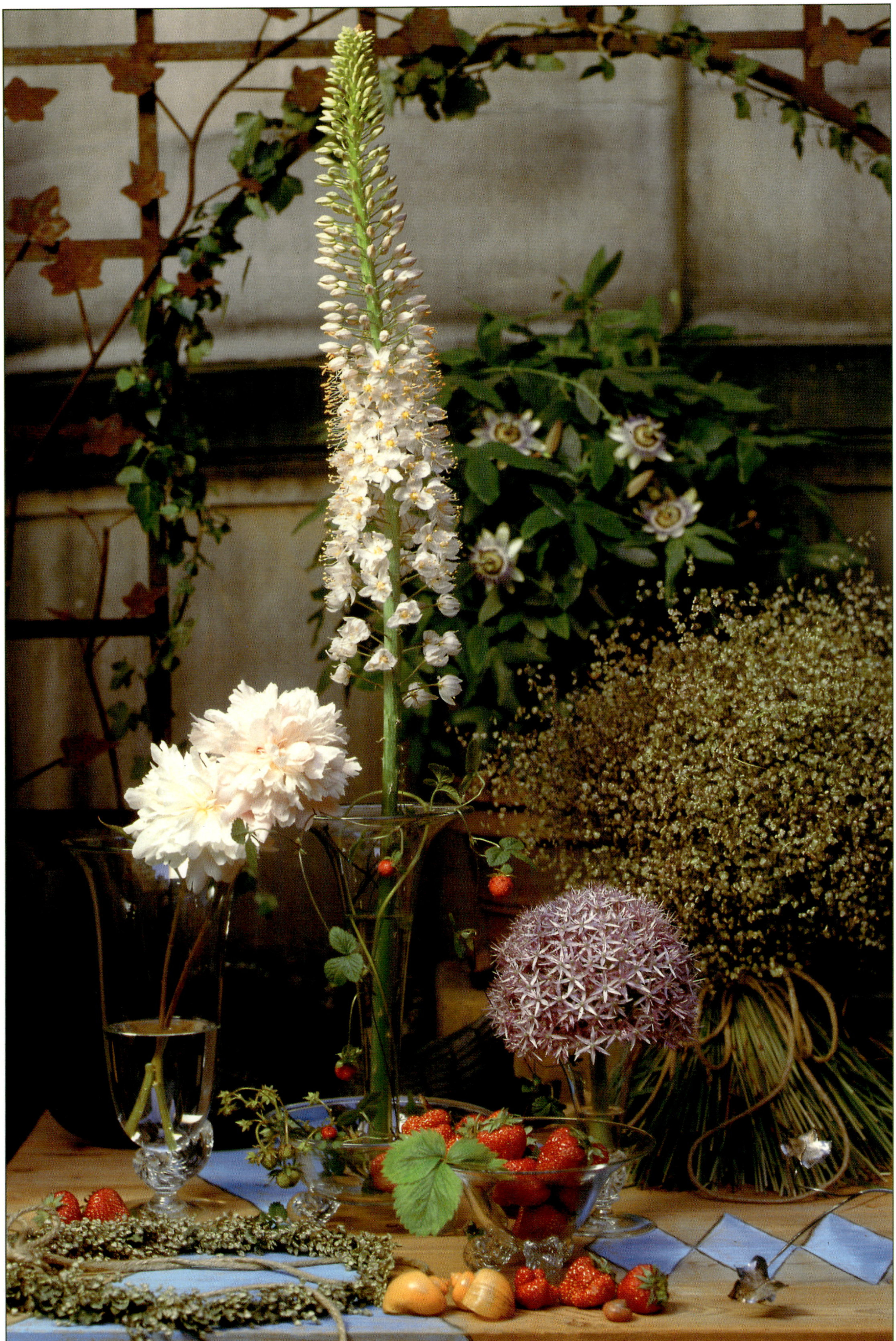

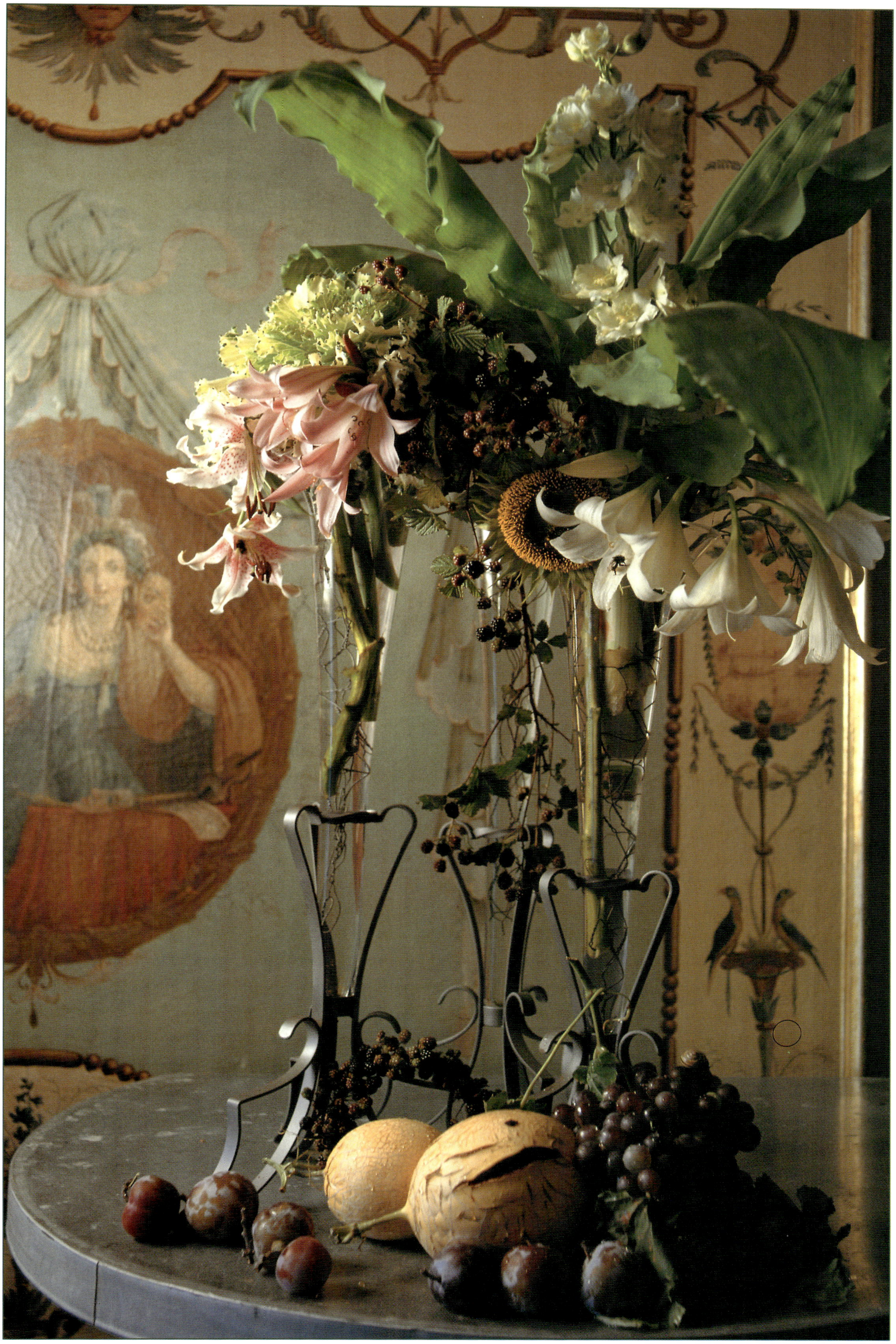

For a while, I amused myself by creating pictures of the seasons – we called the series Picture of the Month, *where you could distinctly discern to which month the picture belonged from the choice of flowers and fruit, etc. We did not, unfortunately, complete a whole year but here are some of the months; June on page 60, September on page 61 and October on page 63.*
On this page is a detail of the September picture, which is probably the one picture closest to my heart.

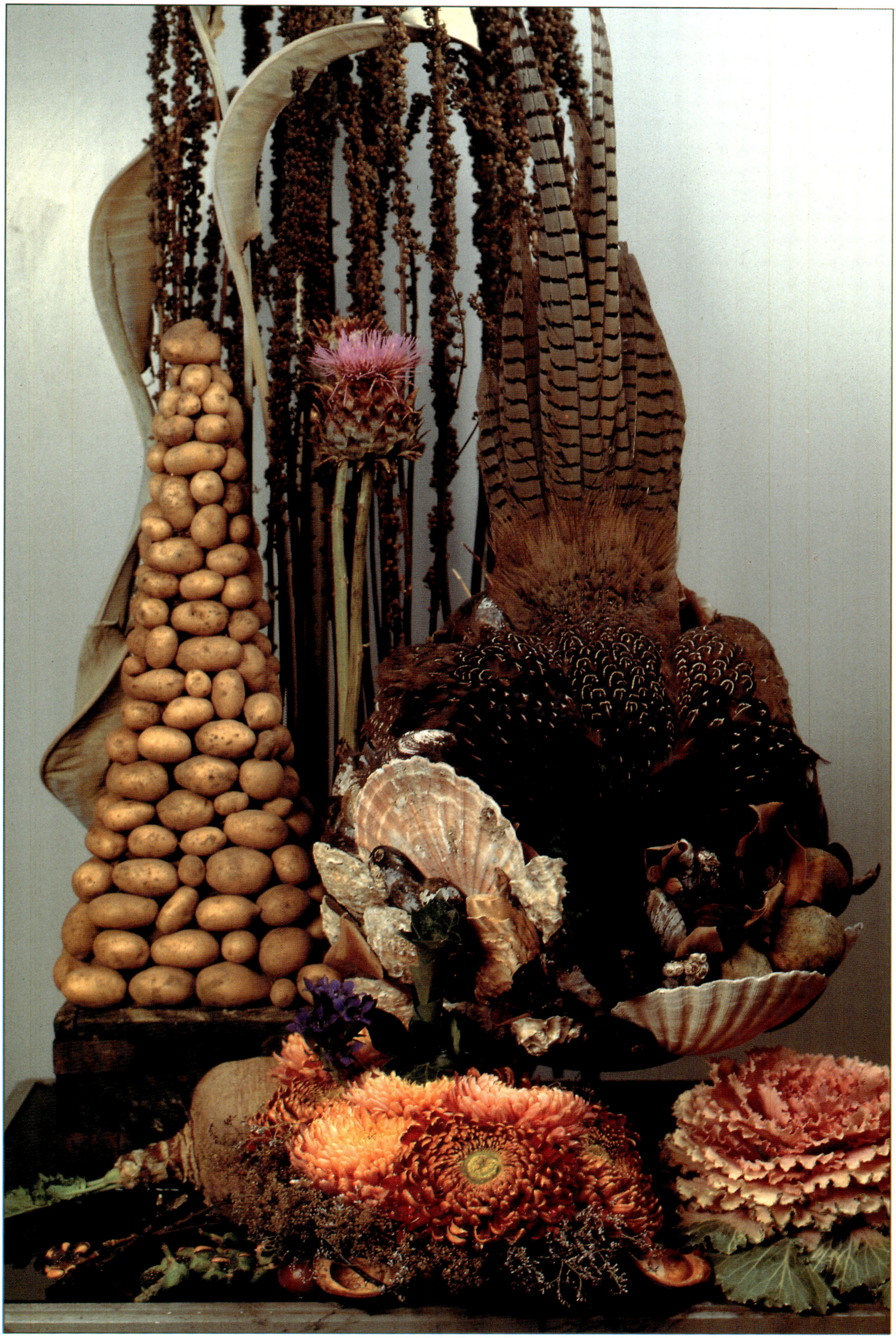

The picture to the right is an example of some of my more baroque juxtapositions.

65

One of my early chandeliers. It often amuses me to »graft« articles used earlier on to »new« effects in my creations. Here parts from chandeliers of Venetian crystal.

The picture to the right is an example of some of my more baroque juxtapositions.

The tabletop earlier served as a front door.

Memories of an eventful life.

Detail from the Karen Blixen basket.

This juxtaposition I have always called Masquerade.

Detail from the exhibition in Brandt's Pakhus 1985.

Mistletoe with scallops.

Picture without text.

One of my commemorative windows on Kongens Nytorv; this time for the 100th anniversary of Karen Blixen's birth.

An example of a perpetual tree, a »dead« camellia plant reconstructed with blooms from the same family.

Top: an avenue of tapestry trees.

Part of the decoration of St. Alban's Church in Copenhagen. I have added a cupola to the pulpit, a wire construction intertwined with carnations and ivy-leaves.

Leaf decoration of a pillar (one perhaps senses a trumpet fanfare).

Also on this page, cupolas and pillars but this time as »serial photo« from my studio on Kongens Nytorv.

The bridal bouquet for the witch herself on Midsummer Night. Amongst other things, the bouquet contains delphiniums and pitcher plants, arum lilies and hemlock, datura and passion-flowers as well as flaming cactus flowers.
The witch was in black.

Midsommernatten 1984

Poster from one of my exhibitions, my first one-man show in Brandt's Pakhus, Copenhagen, spring 1985.

The exhibition was spread over two floors.

On the next page:
Fertility symbol: preserved eggs borne on the backs of eight sheep.

Dove on a cloud regarding its kin in the spherical aviary in the picture to the right.

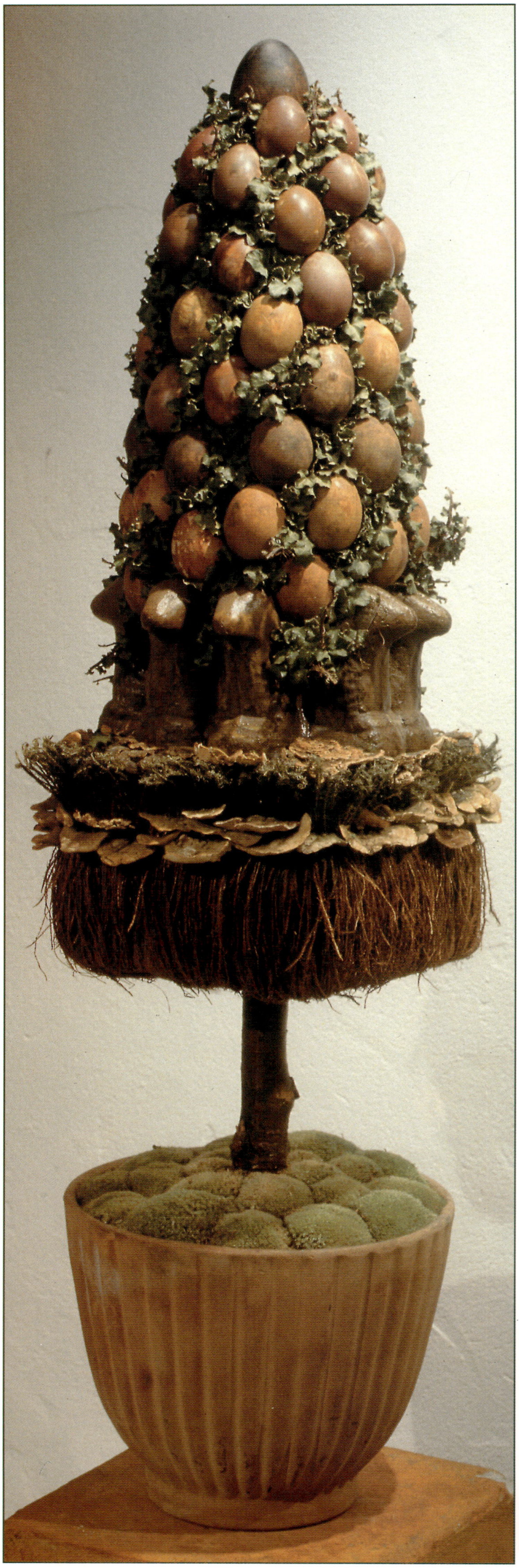
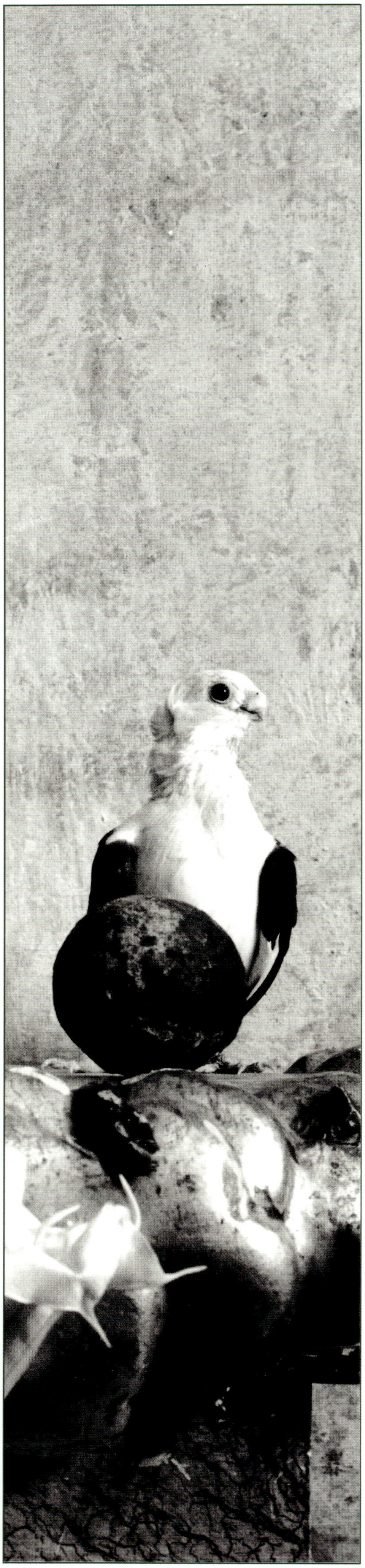
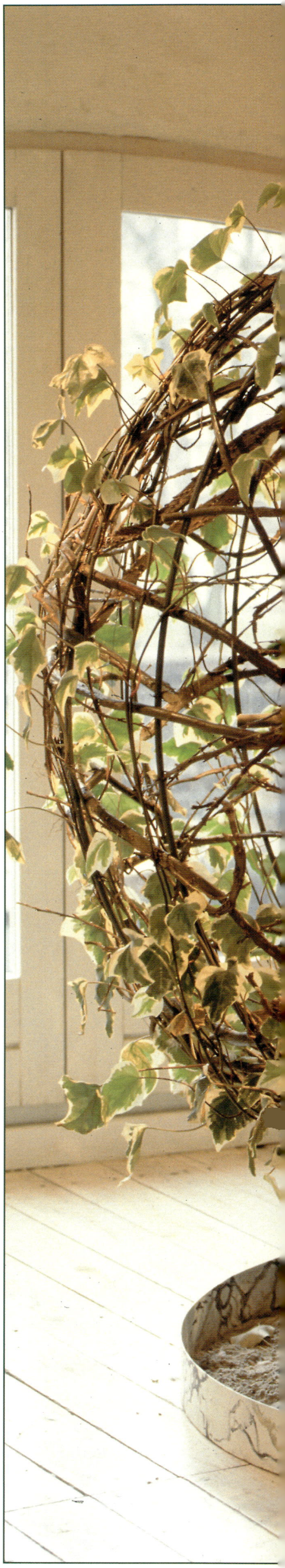

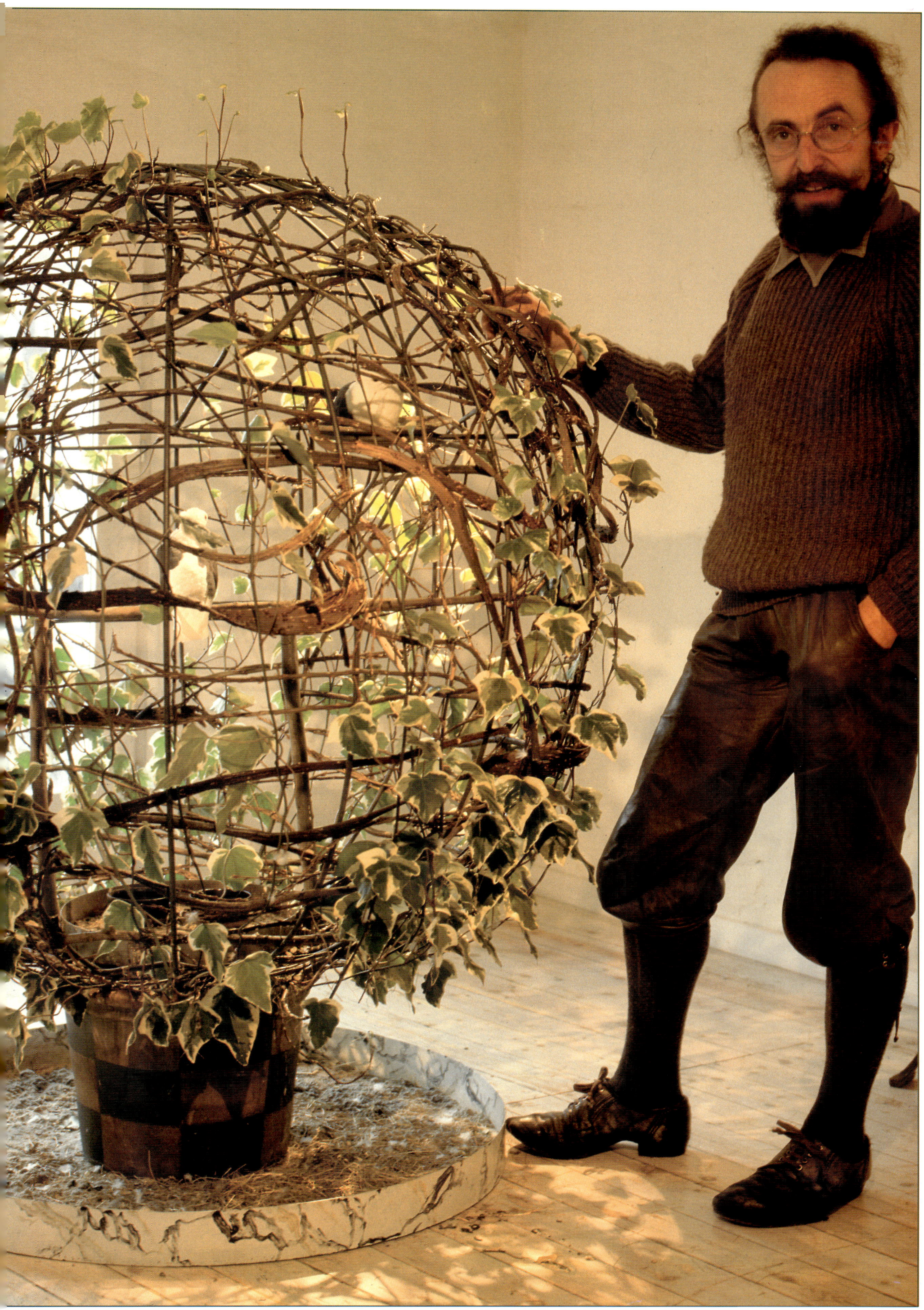

A royal wedding, this time that of circus queen Diana Benneweis. Besides the decorations in the Circus Building, with eight metres high spears with mimosa, which can be seen in the picture to the right, I also created the wedding cake for the 300 guests. The lowest tier was a dummy followed by the cake itself on horseback.

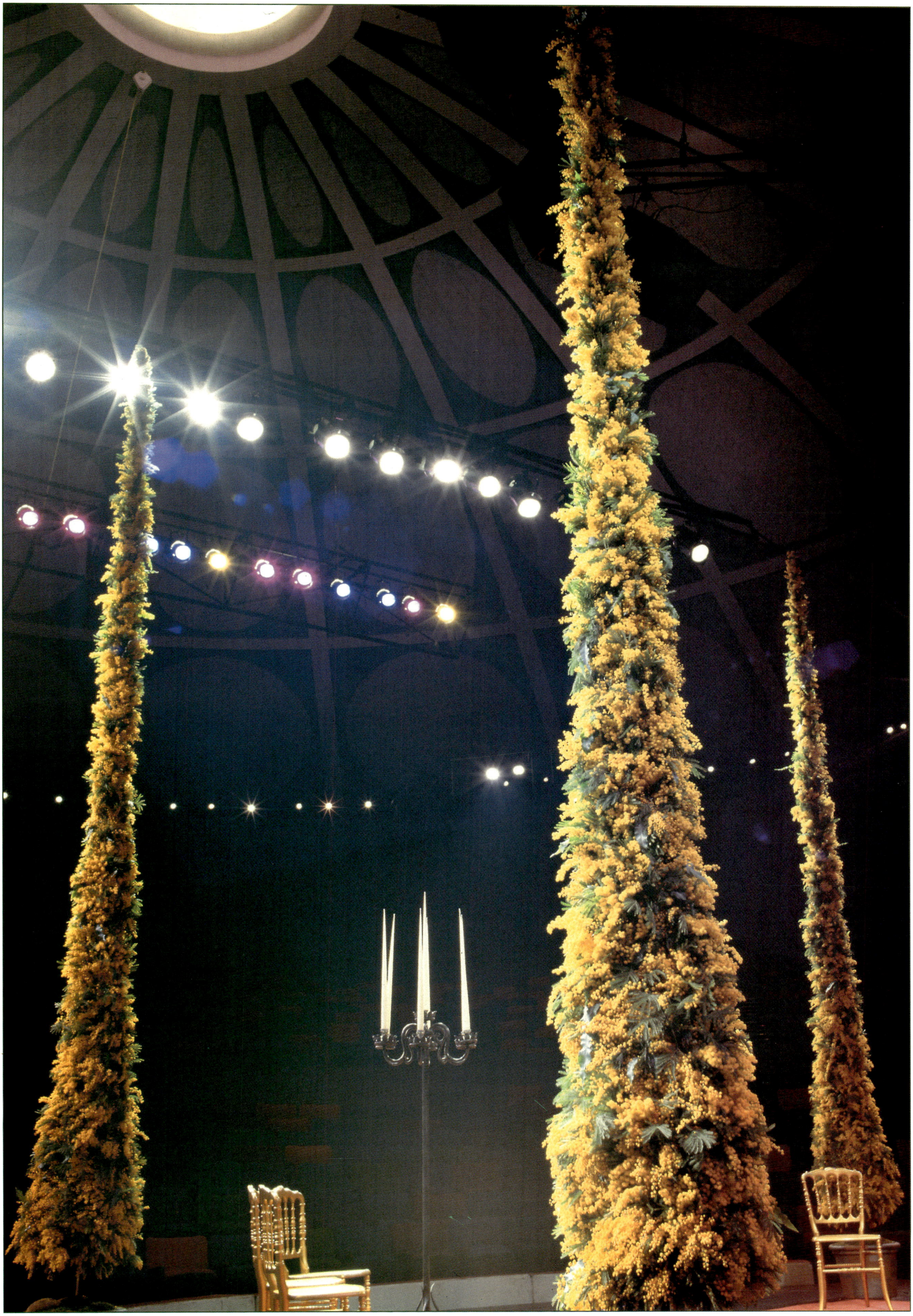

Picture of the atmosphere in my private accomodation in the mid-eighties, with a view on to Kongens Nytorv.

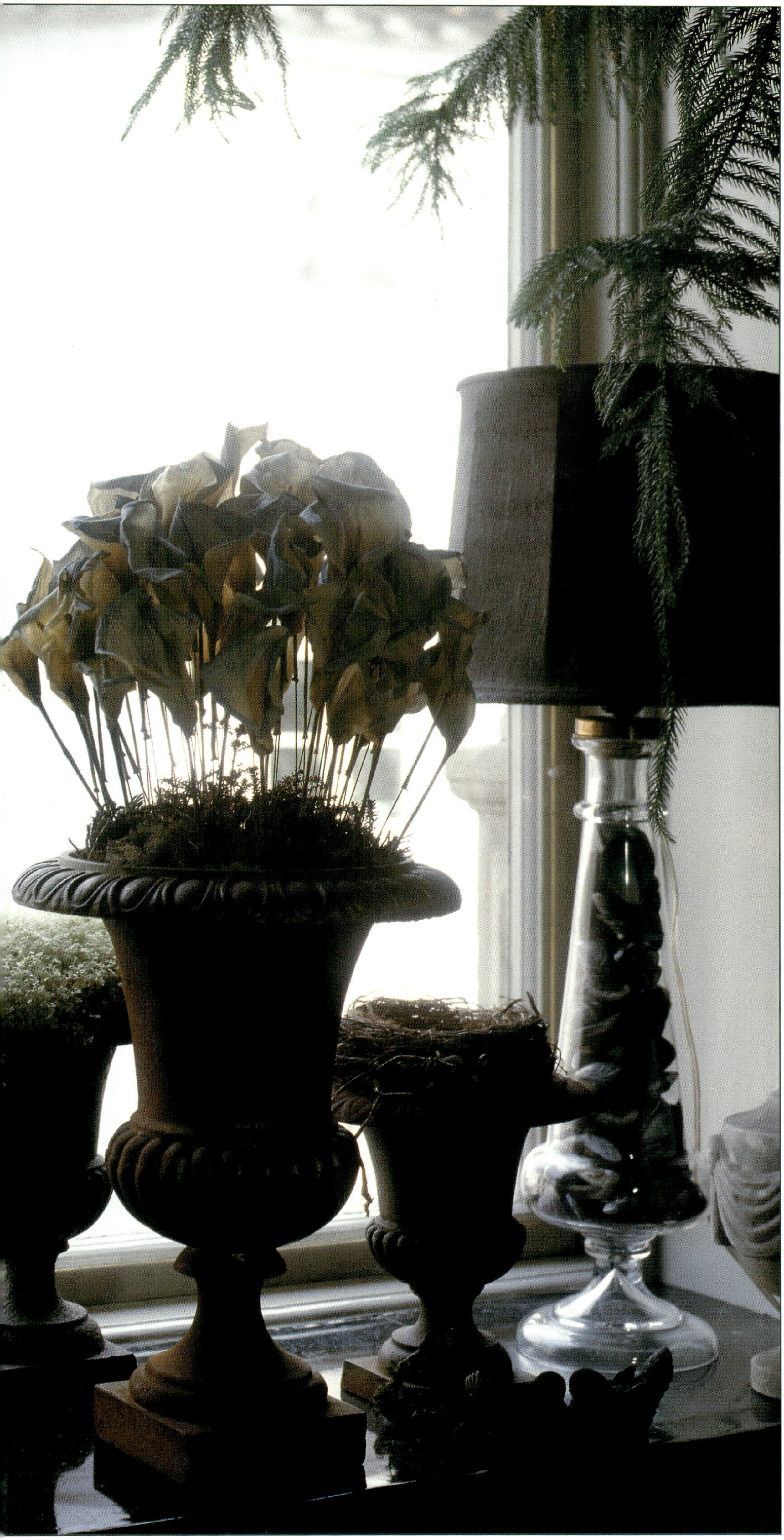

On these and the following pages; more details from my own house:
Top left: collage with pressed lilies.
Bottom left: Here it is the frame that I have chosen to work upon. The outer frame is laid with olive-green leaves, whilst the passepartout is covered in rose-grey silk.
In the picture above: one of two semi-consoles, with the central panel hanging on the wall. For banquets, the panel is used as a dining-table (picture to the right).

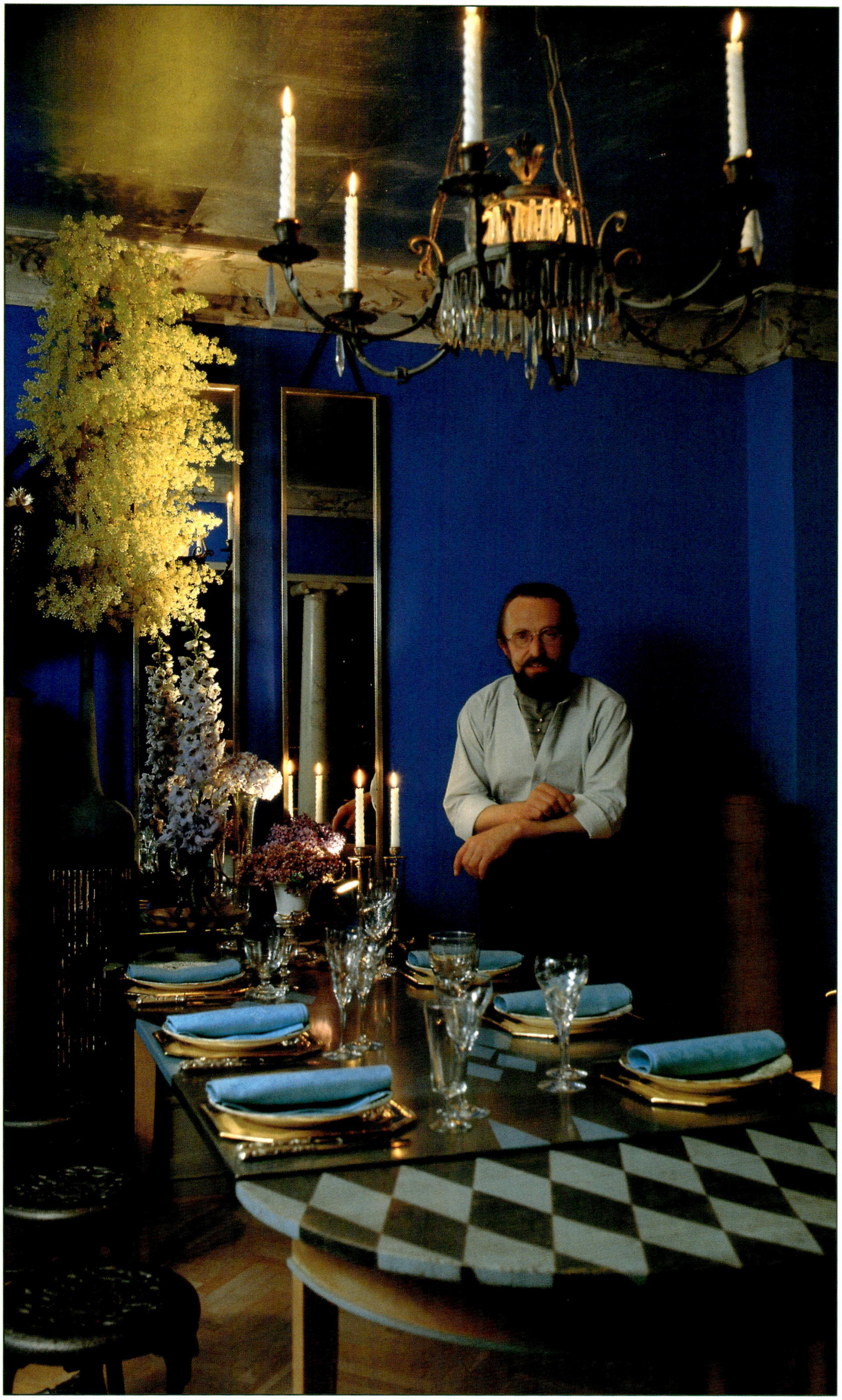

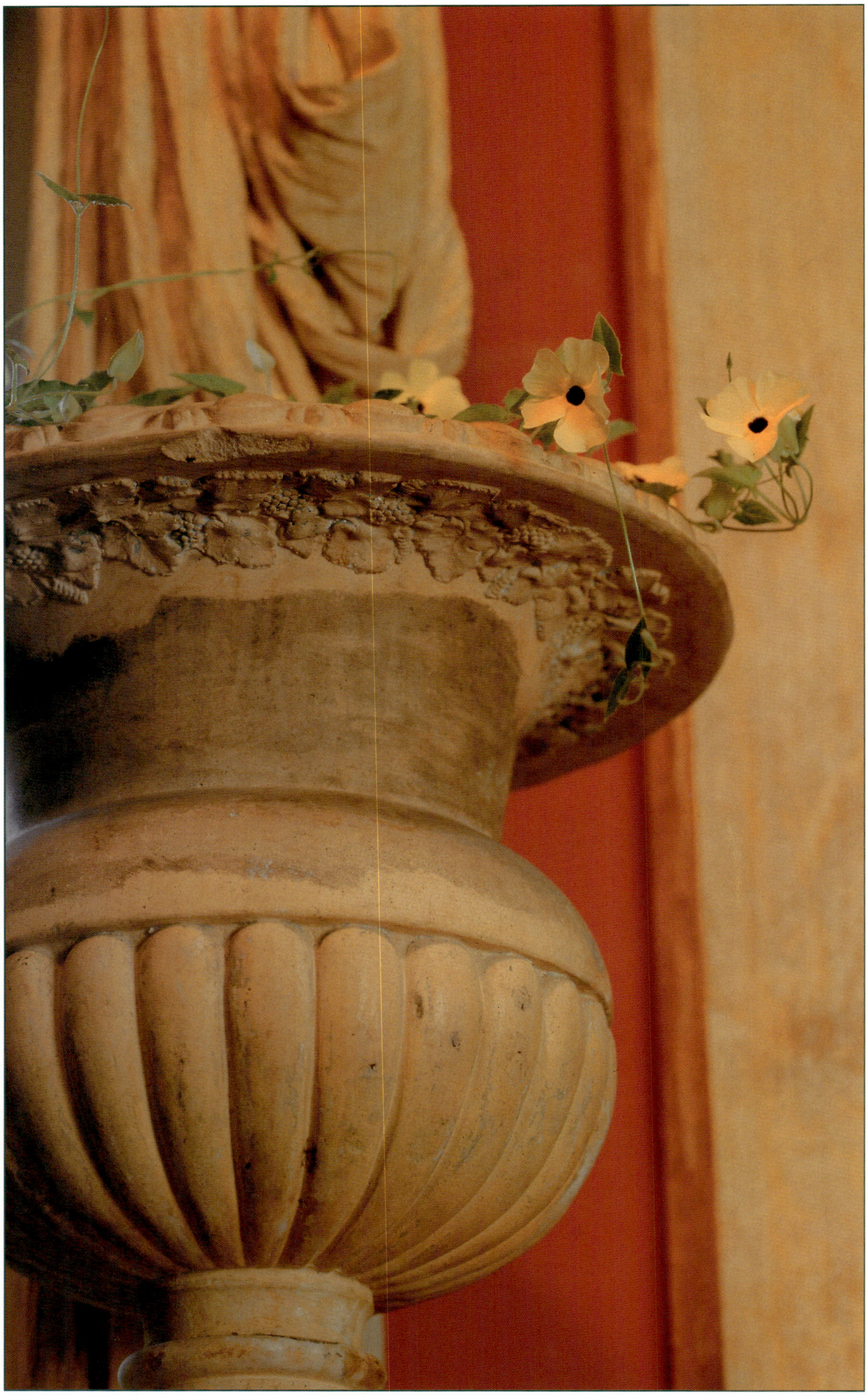

A view into my garden-room. It was situated on the third floor, but I had to have a garden-room which I ostentatiously placed in the darkest room of the appartment. Yet I achieved an exotic atmosphere. The jar on the left photo is produced by Höganäs and is one of my private treasures.

These and the following pages are from my exhibition at Bakkehus Museum in the autumn of 1985. With my things, I attempted to create the life and the atmosphere I imagine existed in the Rahbek home in Bakkehus, when that literary family lived there in the early 1800s.

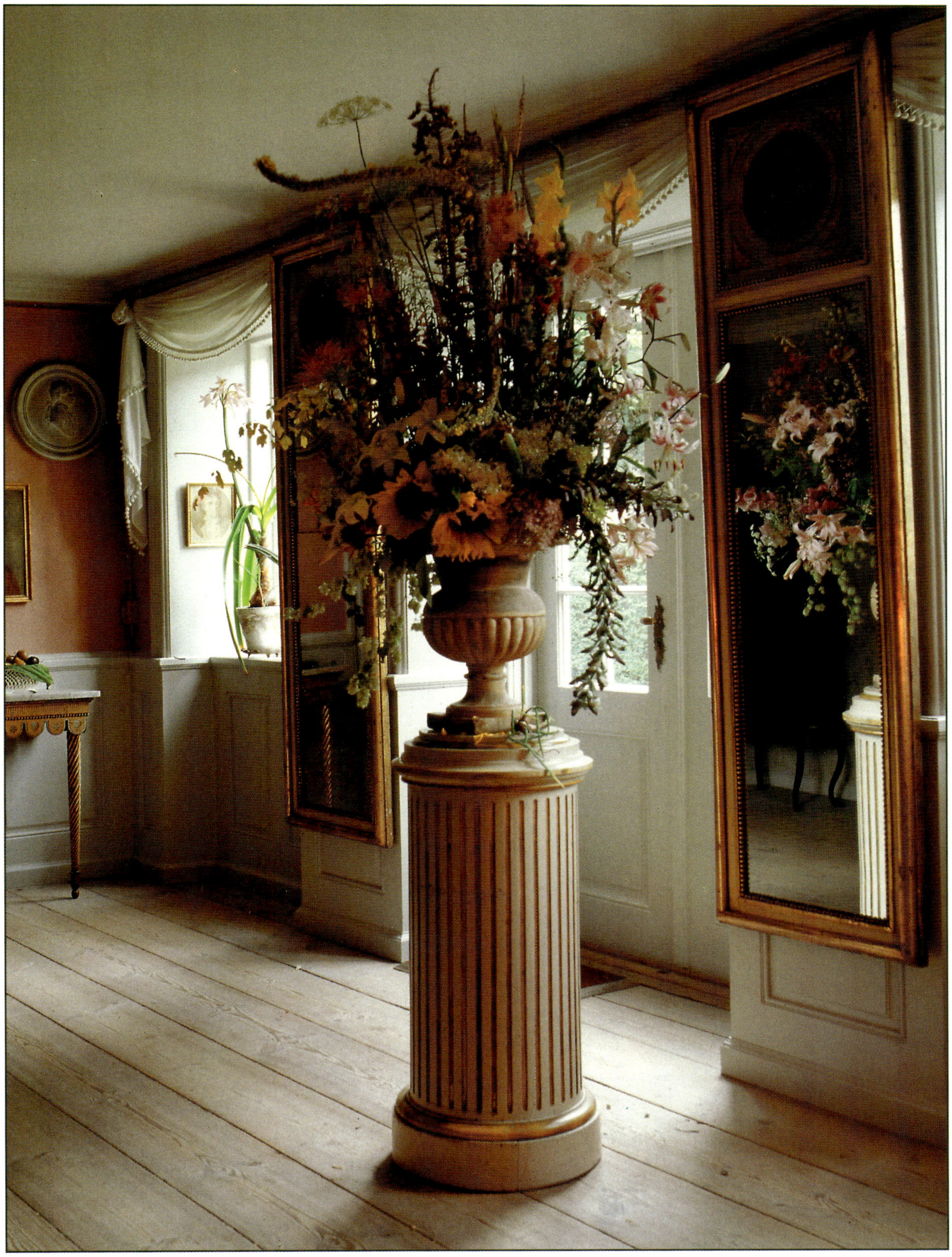

Romantic perspective picture with black swans and exotic carnations. Could have been inspired by Hans Christian Andersen's paper cutouts. Bakkehus Museum 1985.

Porcelain bowl with white and gold flowers. My goal was to create a unity with the pictures hanging behind. Bakkehus Museum 1985.

Window with plants from the period.

Royal Copenhagen Porcelain vases decorated with Cobaea scandens *flowers flanking a bust of the poet Adam Oehlenschläger.*
Bakkehus Museum 1985.

On the way to a theatrical first-night.

Christmas arrangement with pigs and pine-cone mice.
Dummy cakes containing petits fours.

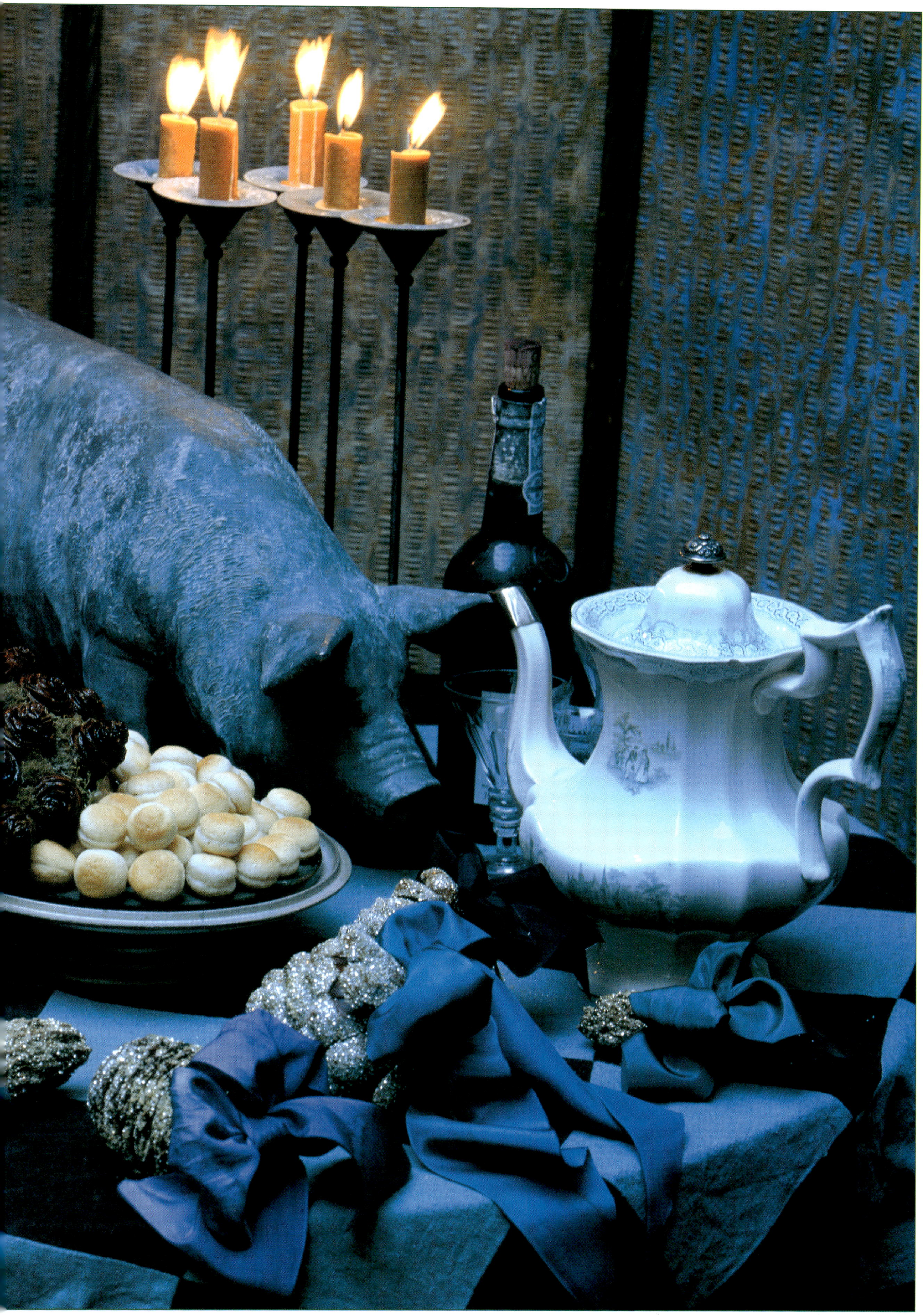

96

The Christmas period has always been one of the times when I have amused myself most. Here I have taken up some confectioner's ideas, like these dummy dessert cakes, which have, however, detachable lids and contain all sorts of edible delights corresponding to the exterior.

The idea was that the dessert would be used as a table decoration and only as the meal was ending would the edible contents be revealed.

The dessert below was a gift to Queen Margrethe and contained candied clementines. I think this was Christmas 1986.

Candied clementines.
Sugar water is boiled and then cooled to 36°C. Clementines are cleaned and dried and placed in the sugar water for 24 hours. They are then taken out and placed to dry for 24 hours. Afterwards the sugar water is again boiled and brought down to 36°C. The fruit are placed in the sugar water for another 24 hours, then dried for 24 hours and are then ready for use.

*A chandelier with a diameter of 130 cm, made of combined fruits of the sea and the garden together with crystals from an earlier chandelier. It reflects elegantly in the silvered ceiling.
One year, I came upon the idea to plait various kinds of branches so that they formed a giant cone, the point of which hovered over the floor. Afterwards I decorated it with my oldest and dearest Christmas decorations and, in addition, gifts that I had received throughout the year. And there the Christmas tree was in the building.*

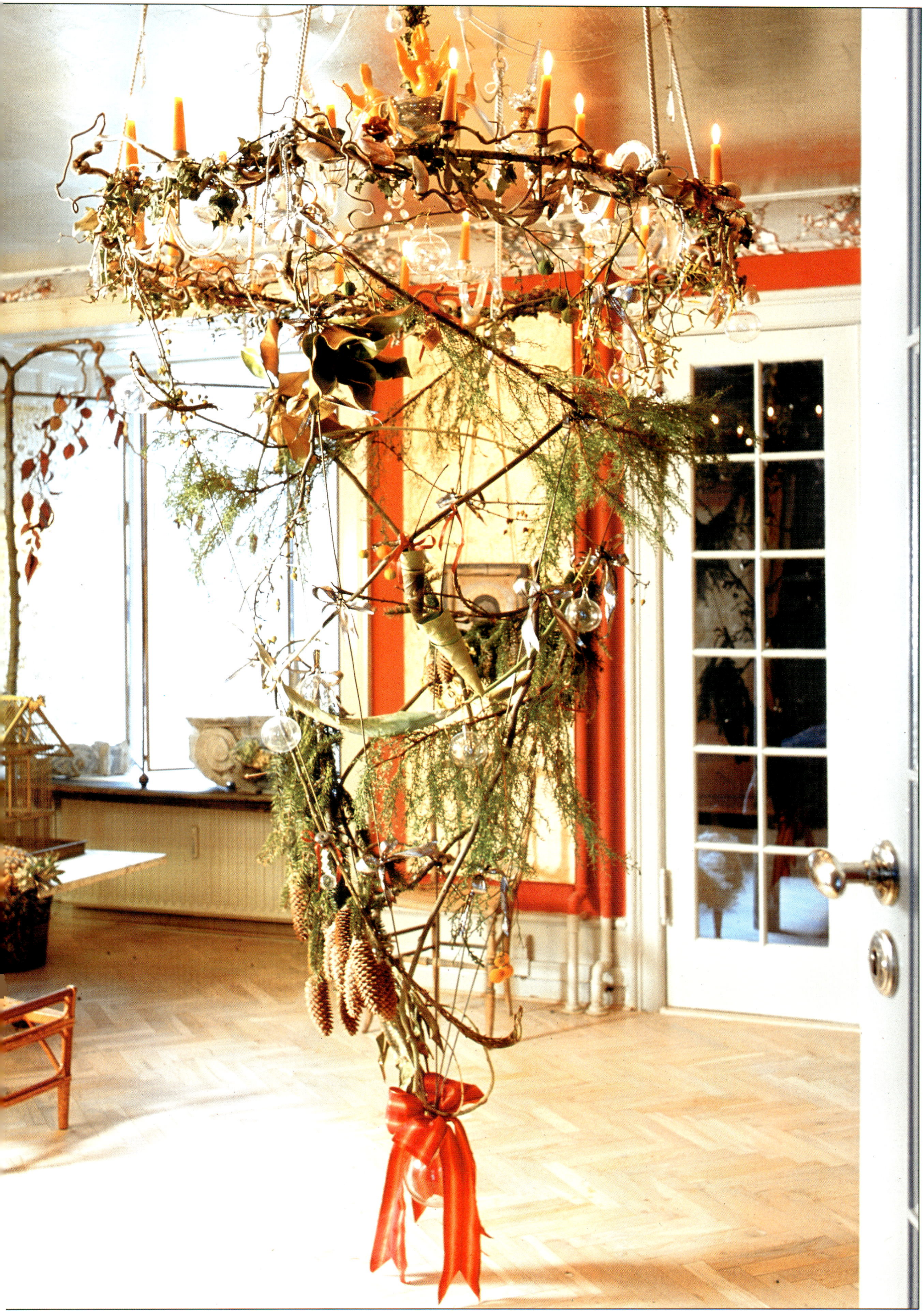

*Like a captain in his craft, I contemplate
from the stairway on Kongens Nytorv
where it should sail. I have received bad
news: notice to leave our famous address.
The year is 1985, and the following year
I could celebrate my tenth anniversary on
Kongens Nytorv.*

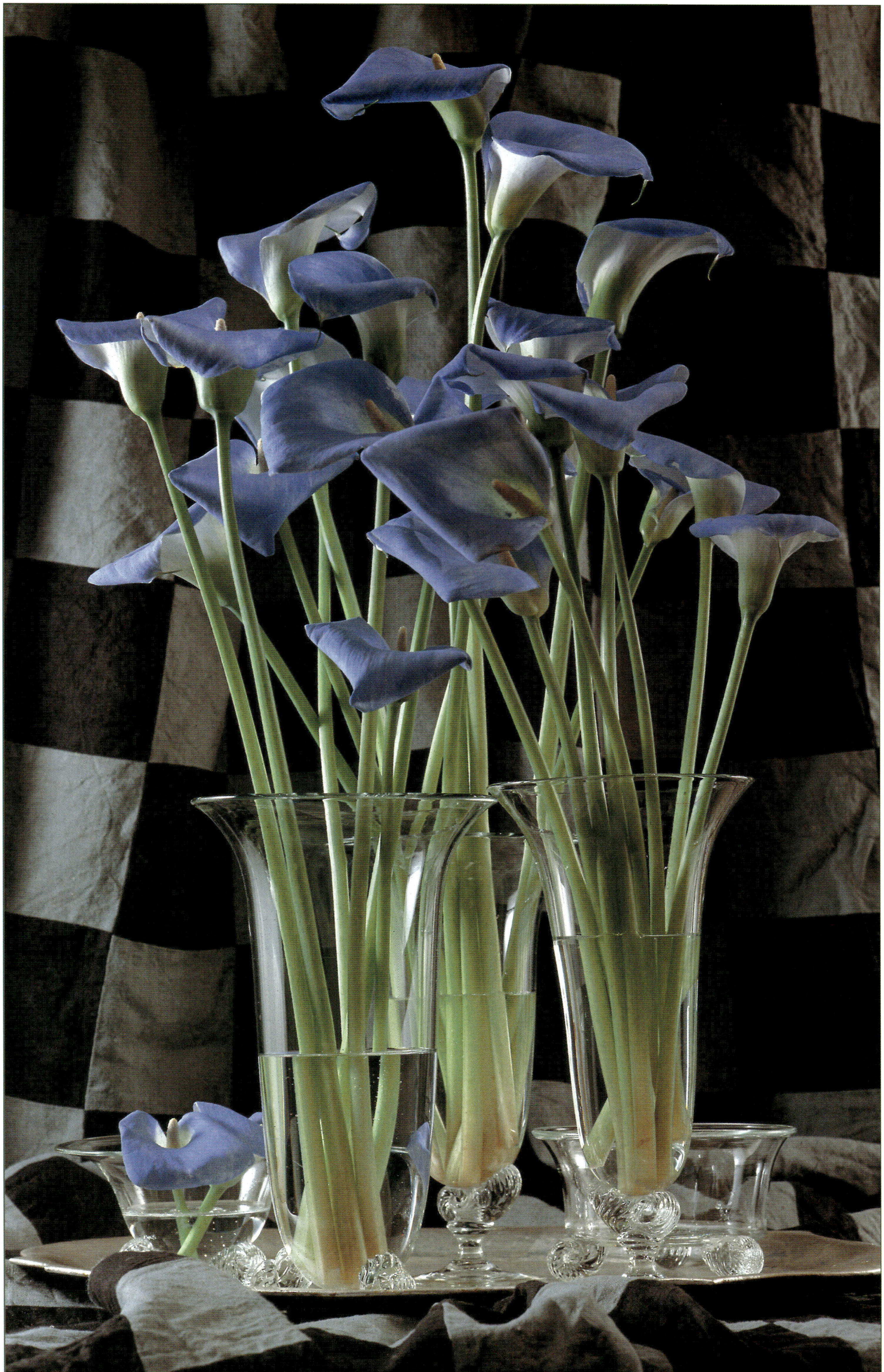

I began a collaboration with the glass artist Darryle Hinz and together we created a series of vases on the occasion of the ten years of the business. One of the vases was a large anniversary goblet with Darryle's Neptune-foot, which was made in 24 signed and numbered examples. 12 of them I gave to 12 of my chosen customers, the remaining 12 we sold from the shop.

The exciting moments when the new shapes come into being. Is there any hope for one's illusions, one is reluctant to compromise?
Glass workshop; Darryle Hinz and Anja Kjær 1985.

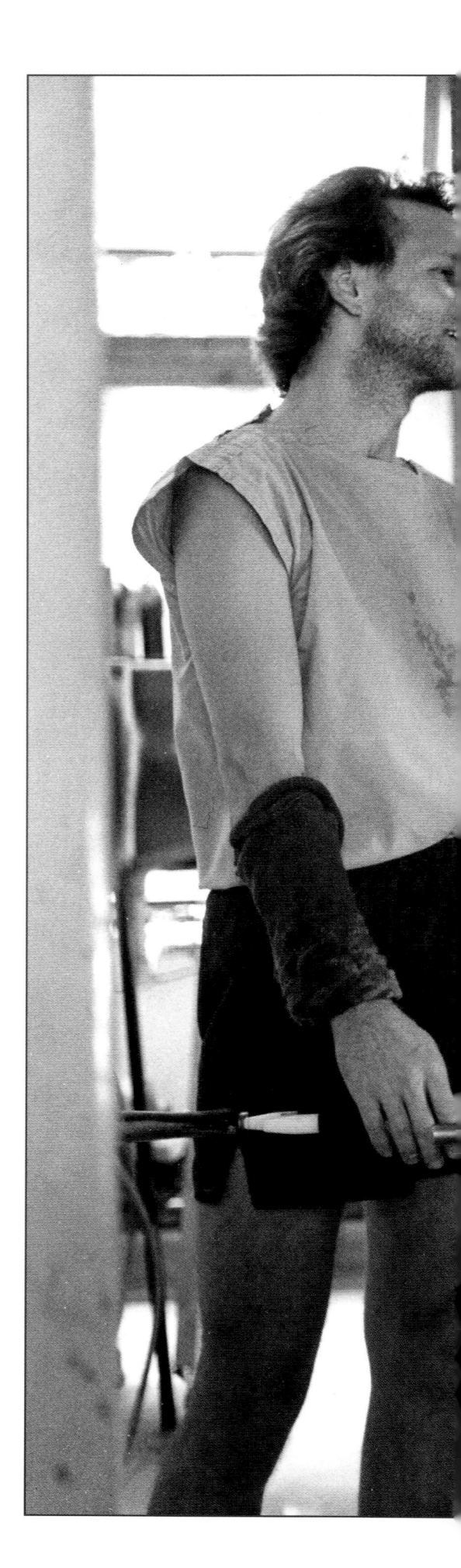

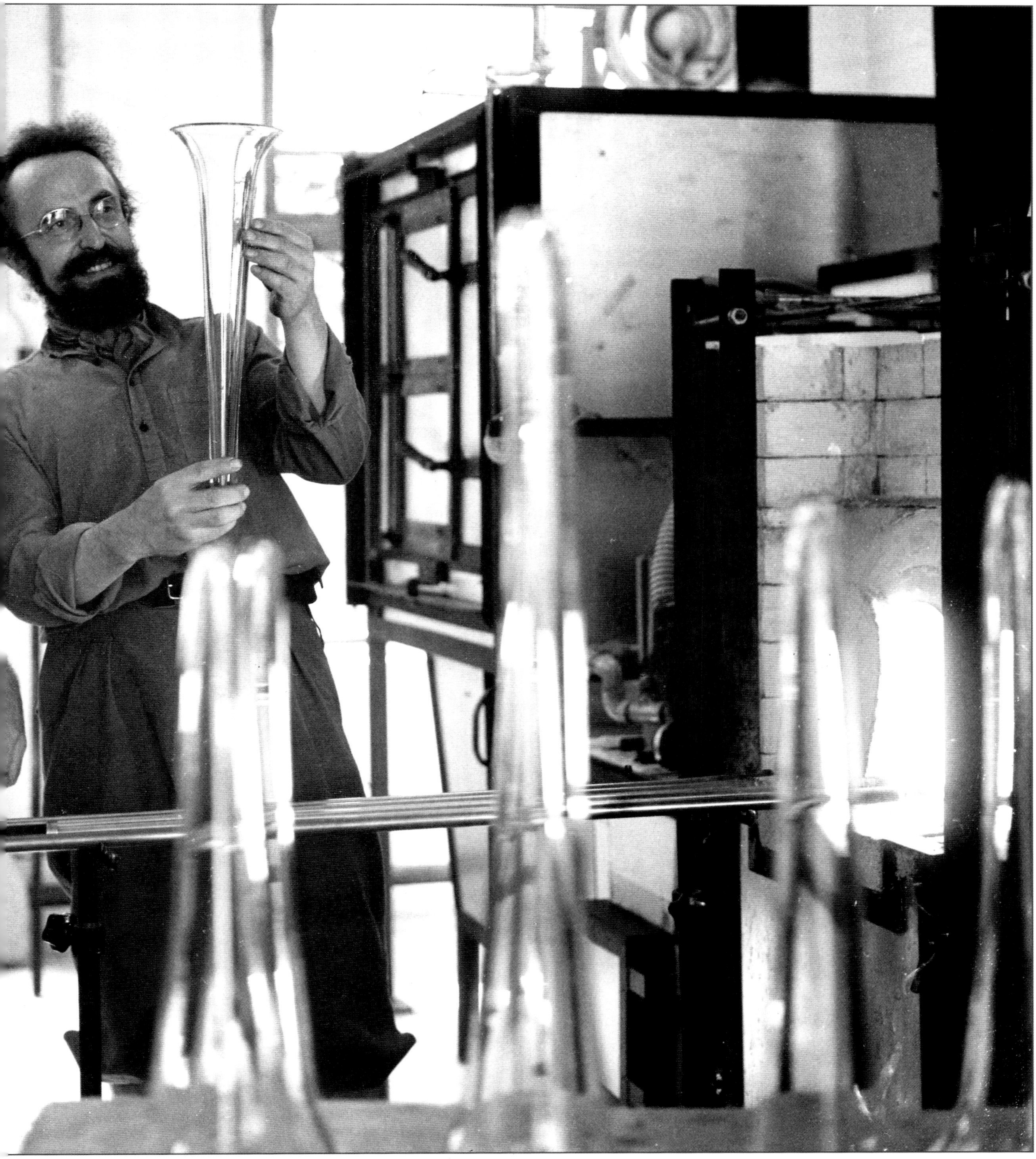

In 1986 we marked our tenth anniversary on Kongens Nytorv with Wondrous Trees, *my largest one-man exhibition hitherto, in the courtyard of Charlottenborg.*
Glimpses from this on pages 106-107, 108-109, 110-111 and 112-113.

The picture shows a commission, a parrot cage for gold-crested cockatoos.

TAGE ANDERSEN

"Forunderlige Træer"
Charlottenborg
Slotsgaard

Udstillingen er åben hver dag fra 10.00-17.00 i perioden 19.-28. september 1986.
Charlottenborg Slotsgaard
Kongens Nytorv

Avenue of trees made of various dyed species of moss. The inspiration was ashlar masonry.

107

Another group of moss trees, here in more comfortable and round forms. The inspiration for the big tree again came from masonry.

In the glass case, Fairy Tale Tree with chequered fritillaries. The pattern of the flowers is strengthened by the chequered base. The lamp has taken on the shape of the tree, the crown (the shade) is made of leaves.

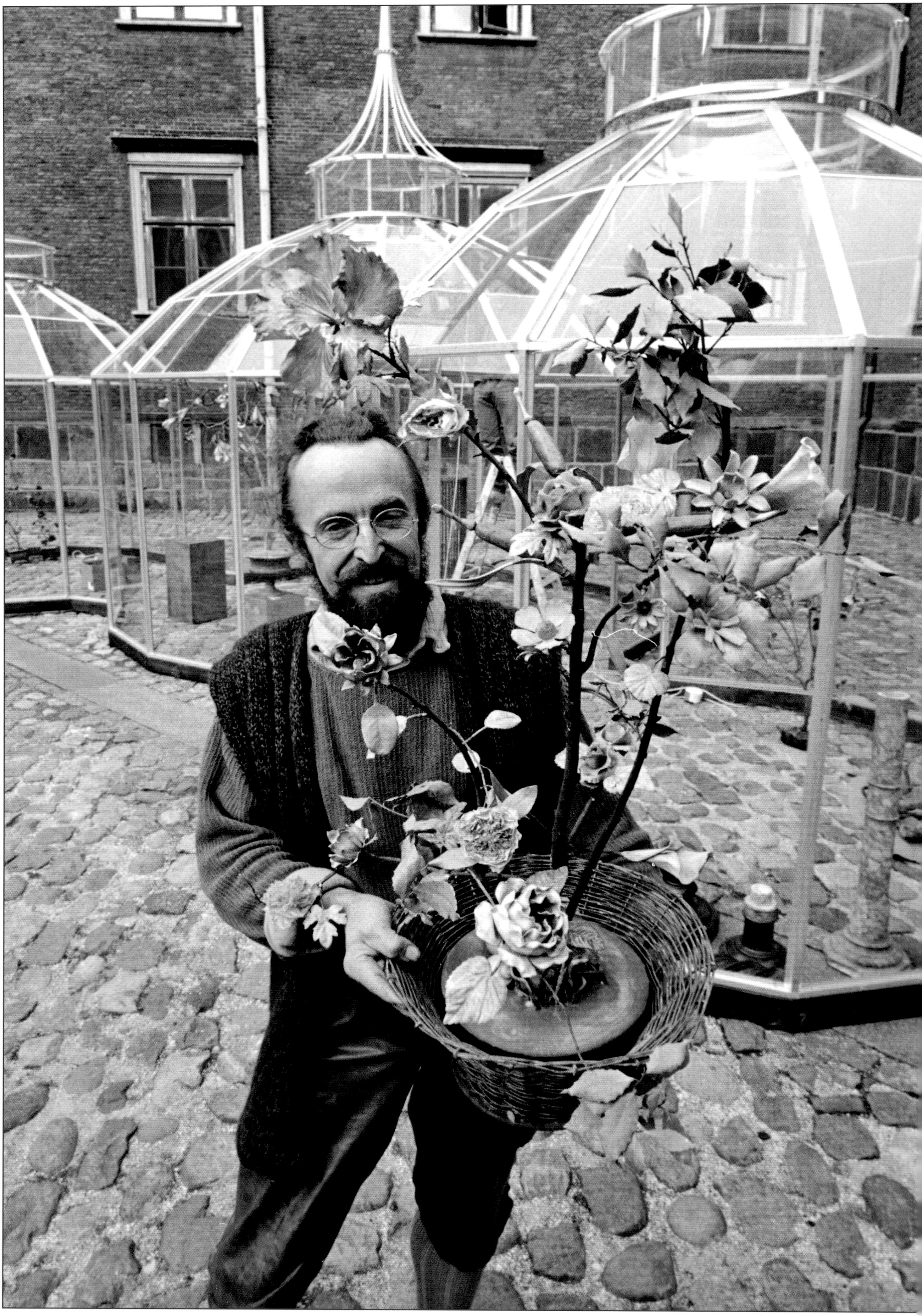

A fantastic peep.

The tree's leaves are made of zinc.

*The exhibition is still under
construction. The tree I am showing
carries all sorts of blooms from
sand-dried hibiscus to roses and irises
in iron and marzipan.*

Pagoda trees, whose form was inspired by antique garden urns, made of honesty. The height is 225 cm.

Twelve and sixteen sided glass pavilions respectively created shelter for the tenderer »growths«. The glass pavilions were from the Jutland firm Classica. In the foreground can be seen a miniature version of Krinsen in the centre of Kongens Nytorv.

*Autumn window on Kongens Nytorv,
1986. The clipped tree is created from
the wild flowersea lavender.*

For a period of three months in 1987, we had a shop in a gateway, partly under the open sky, from whence this picture comes.

Ivy chair, made in six examples for the first time in 1983.

For an ice and fruit bar, I created this motive for a transparent awning to a window on to a courtyard.

*In September 1987, we are able to let
the light stream into the windows of our
new domicile, Ny Adelgade 12,
Copenhagen.*

If I steal a stroll in the late evening, I ask myself is it real or am I dreaming? Yes, reality is also present . . . I shall now be sending my pictures and fairy-tales into the world from here.

We have moved into the fairy-tale.
The period is spring with a selection of
poetic flowers. In, for example, the iron
vase can be seen auriculas and edelweiss.
The lustre-coloured eggs on »sticks« are
one of my fertility symbols and in our
shop a typical sign of spring.

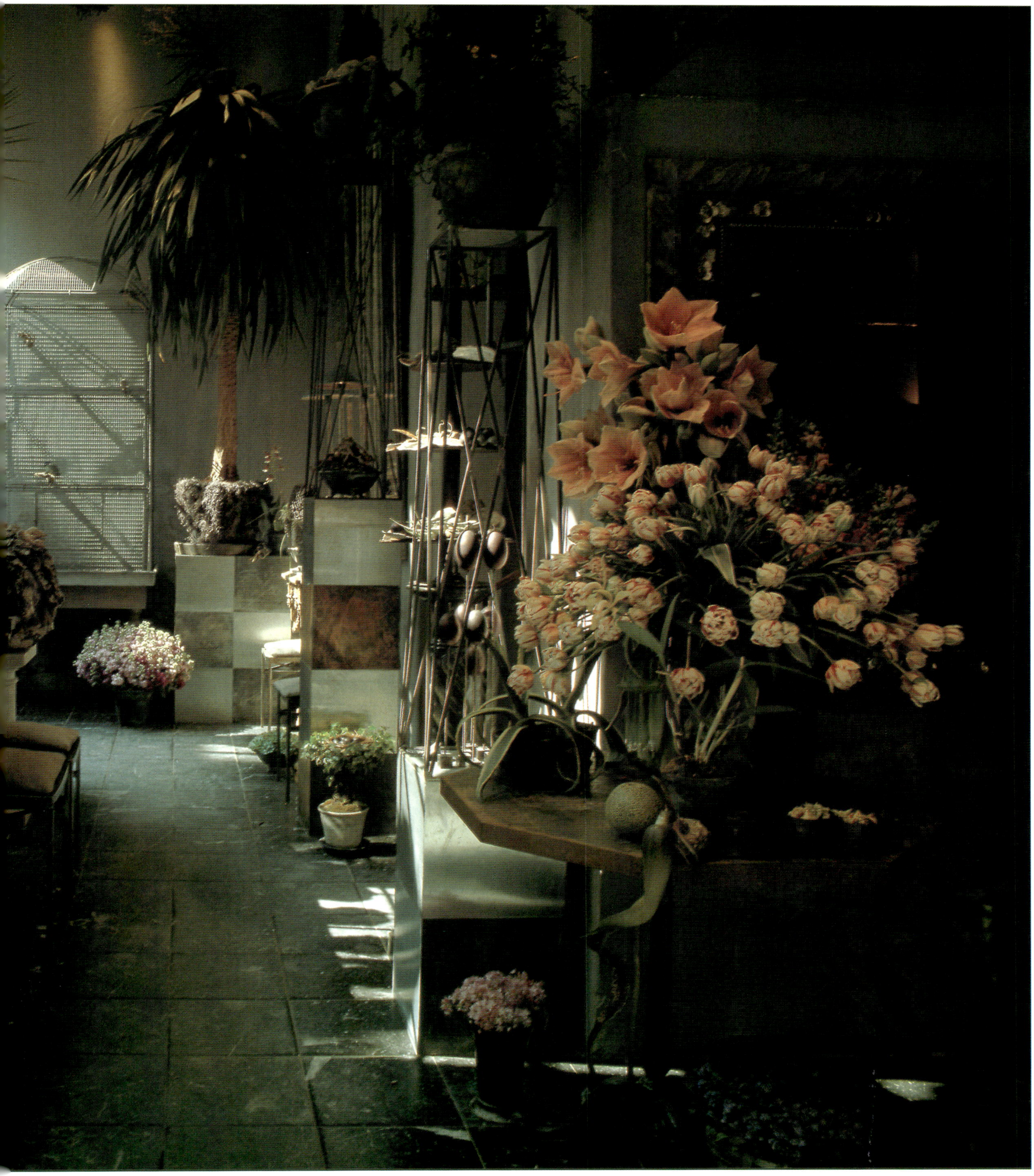

Details from an early summer interior. The square flower chests, called Tivoli chests, here function as vases for mignonette, forget-me-not, asters and scabiosa. An arrangement where even humble flowers now appear as a sculpture. Under the pumpkin on its pedestal can be seen boxes of violets. These mini-hatboxes, with lids and ribbons, are one of our specialities and a typical gift for a loved one.

Three of my very typical creations; at the top, my favourite Lilium regale, *then a combination of red cabbage, hydranga hortensis and* Ondsidium *orchids. To the right, a terracotta pot with modelled doves and ivy leaves, one of the more unique ones, only produced in 12 examples, each of which, however, has its own distinctive features.*

An incredible combination of nature's blemishes, the photographer's skill and the viewer's ability to see . . .

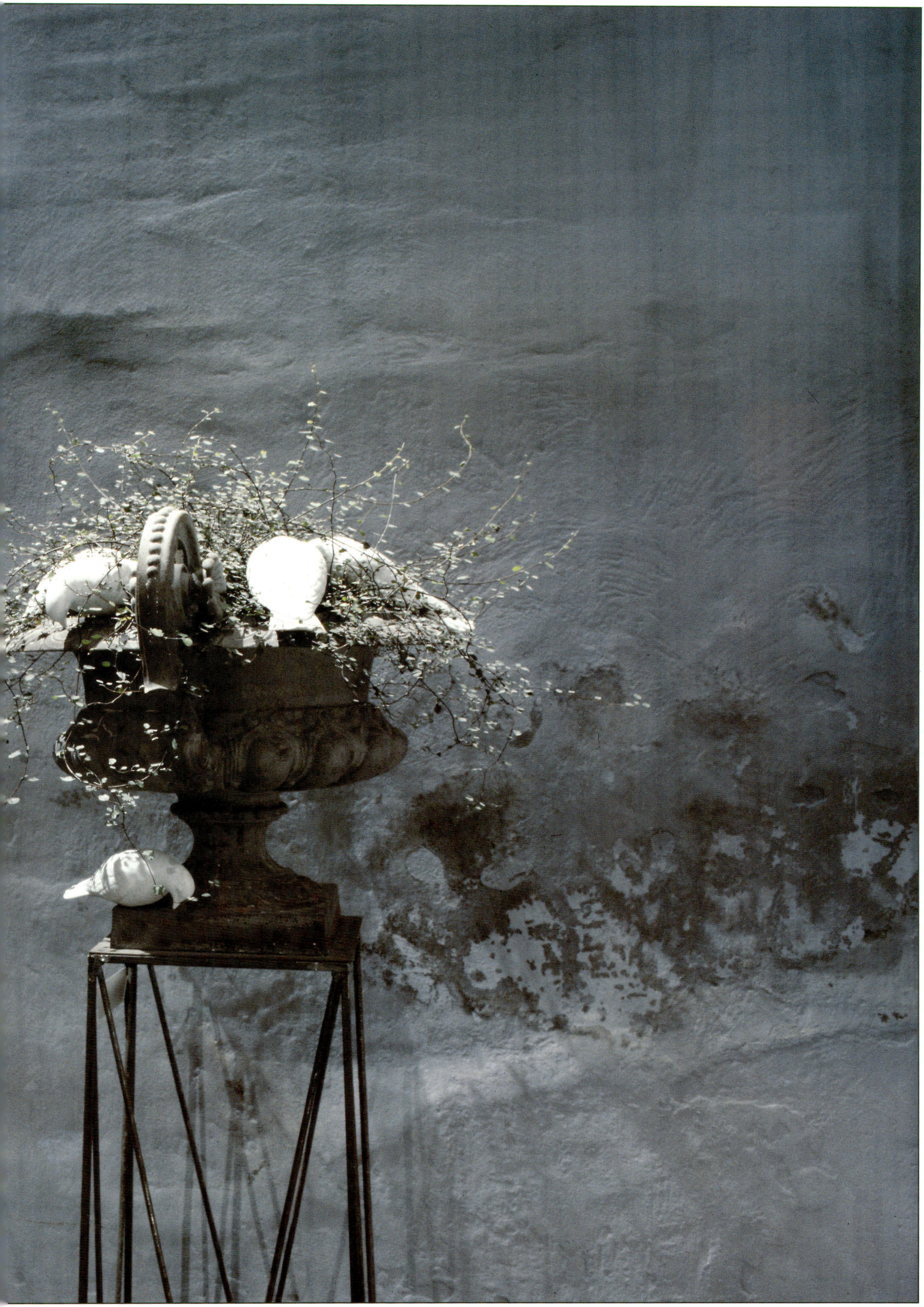

Yet another example, where I have worked with nature and chance as partners. This composition was worked upon for some weeks, in such a way that parts were left to dry, others almost to perish, in order to achieve, by a constant combination of fresh and new things, contrasts between »life and death«. Finally to be worked up pictorially in three dimensions and end in glass cases in the interior pictured on page 209.

My personal interchange has to be between the simple and the strong – and the manifoldness of the details.

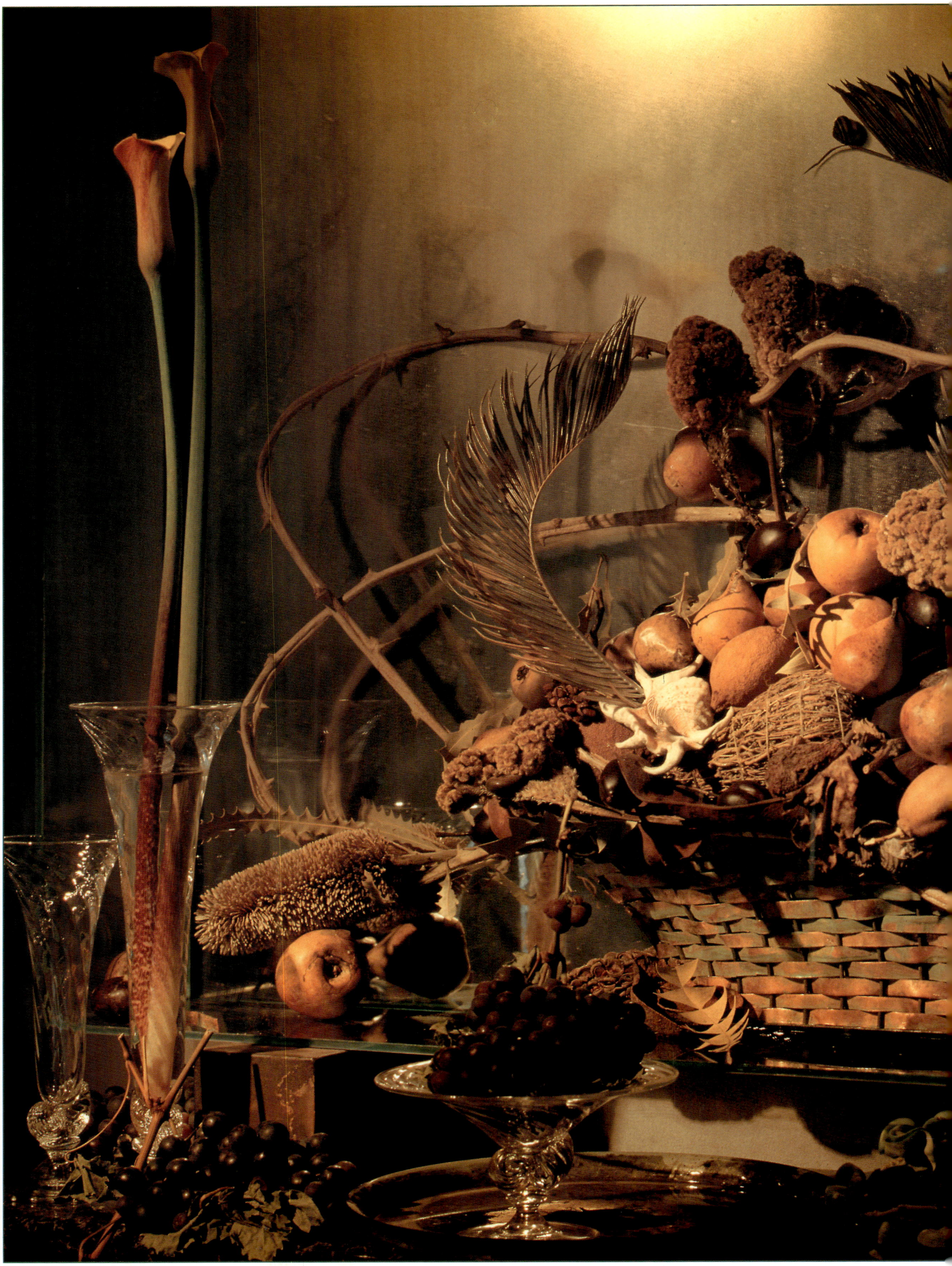

Now and then I have worked with great pleasure on panopticons. Here glass cases with baskets, plaited in copper, full of exotic fruits, partly preserved and partly made from papier maché or sugar.
The arrangement was later included in the decorations of the well-known Restaurant Kong Hans in Copenhagen.

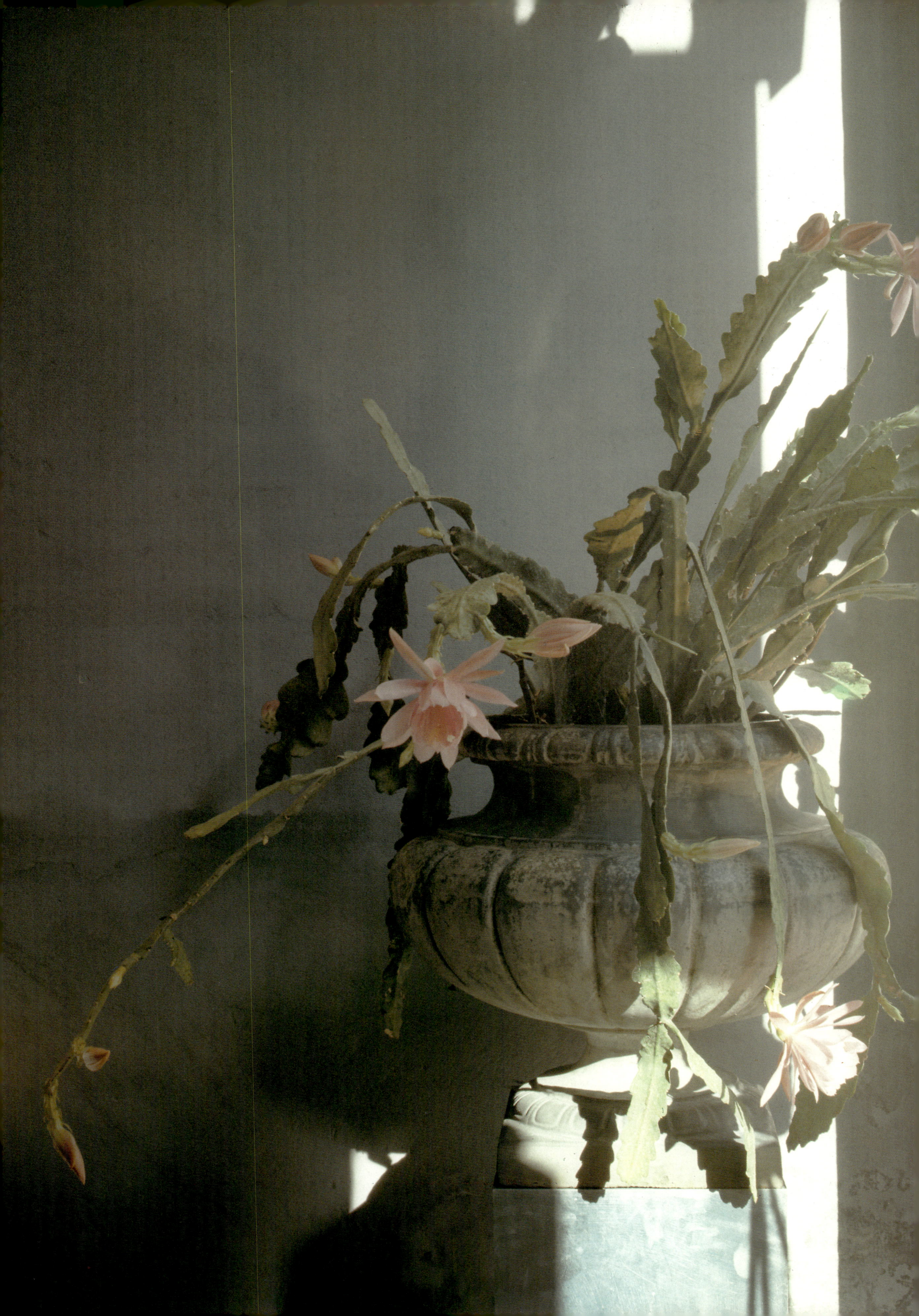

The atmosphere in these arrangements calls for champagne . . .

Pressed pansies gathered in a basket and placed behind glass. On the next page, Datura flowers and cattleya orchids.

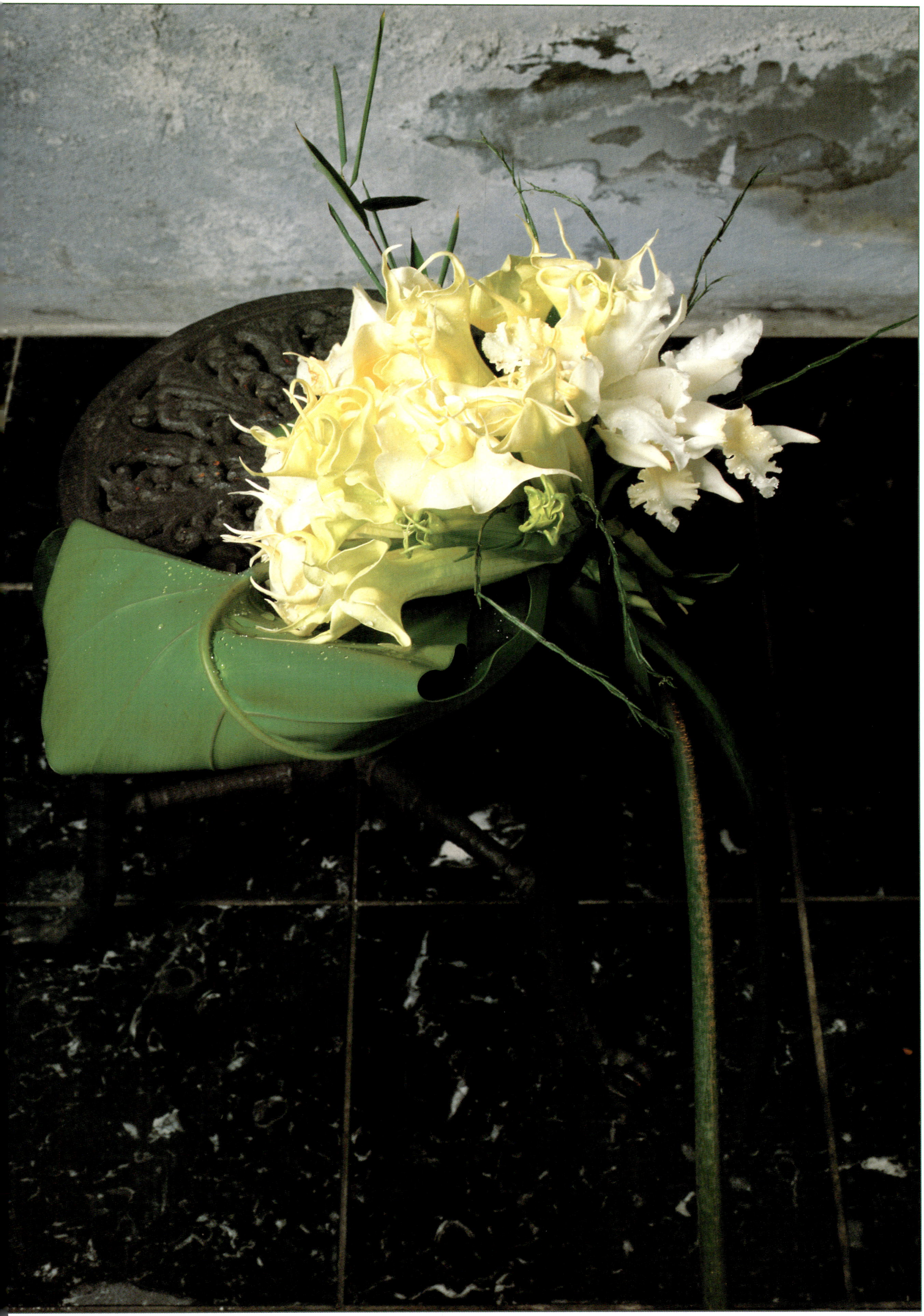

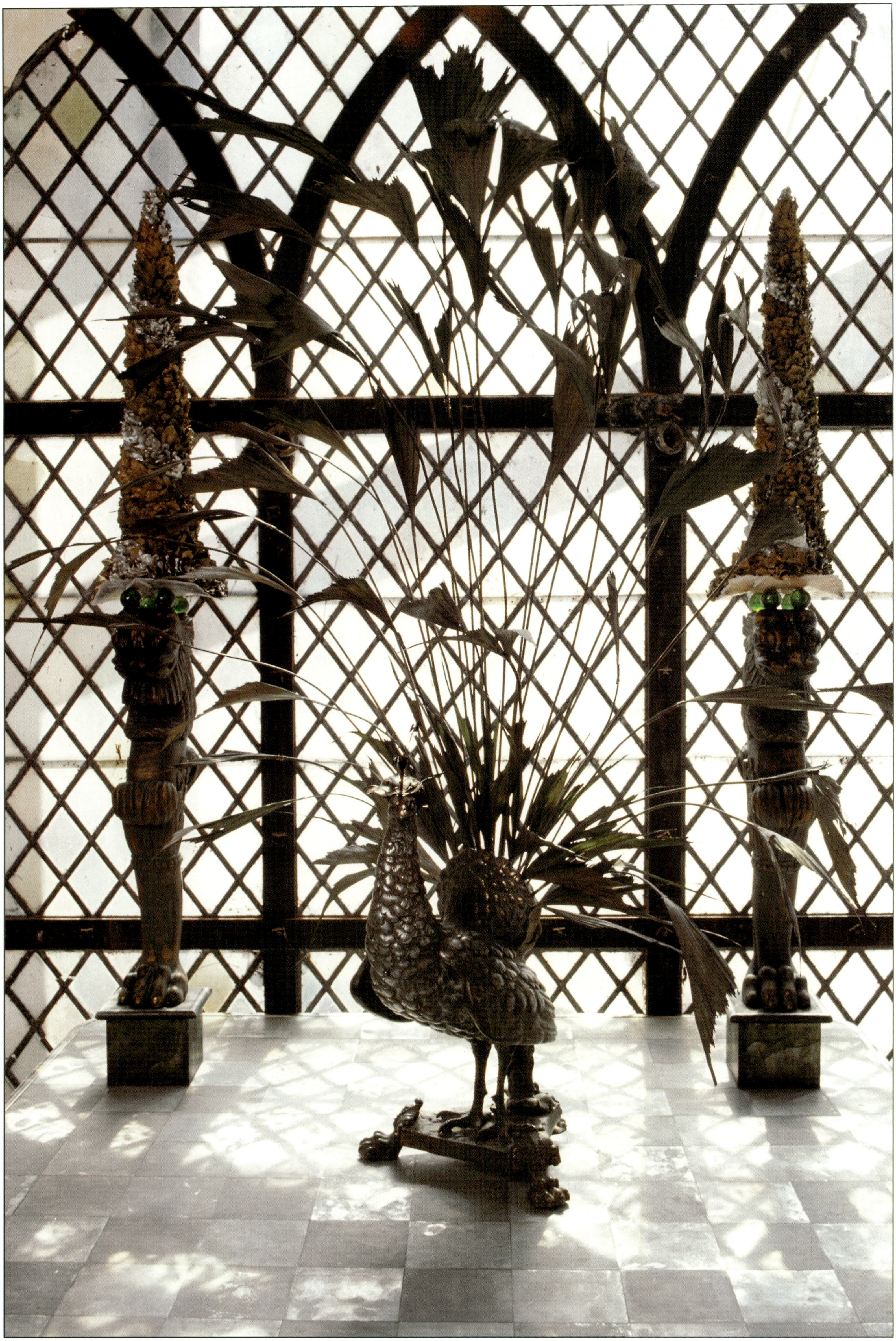

Details from the exhibition at Rosenborg Castle in spring 1987. All the compositions were conceived as show dishes for the table setting in Christian IV's honour, here for example, centrepieces of Indian elephants with fruit.
The fabulous beasts on the previous pages bear centrepieces inspired by the twisted tower of the Copenhagen Stock Exchange. The peacock symbolizes royal pomp.

The Orangery in Holland Park, London, was the frame of my first international one-man exhibition in autumn 1988.
The Orangery inspired me to a new line. We plaited, for example, iron baskets in innumerable models and created birdcages and aviaries, some shaped like large bee-hives, others as angular pavilions.

On the next page, garden aviary with the African cuckoo Turako. The spire on the top is, like the encircling garland, planted with muehlenbeckia.

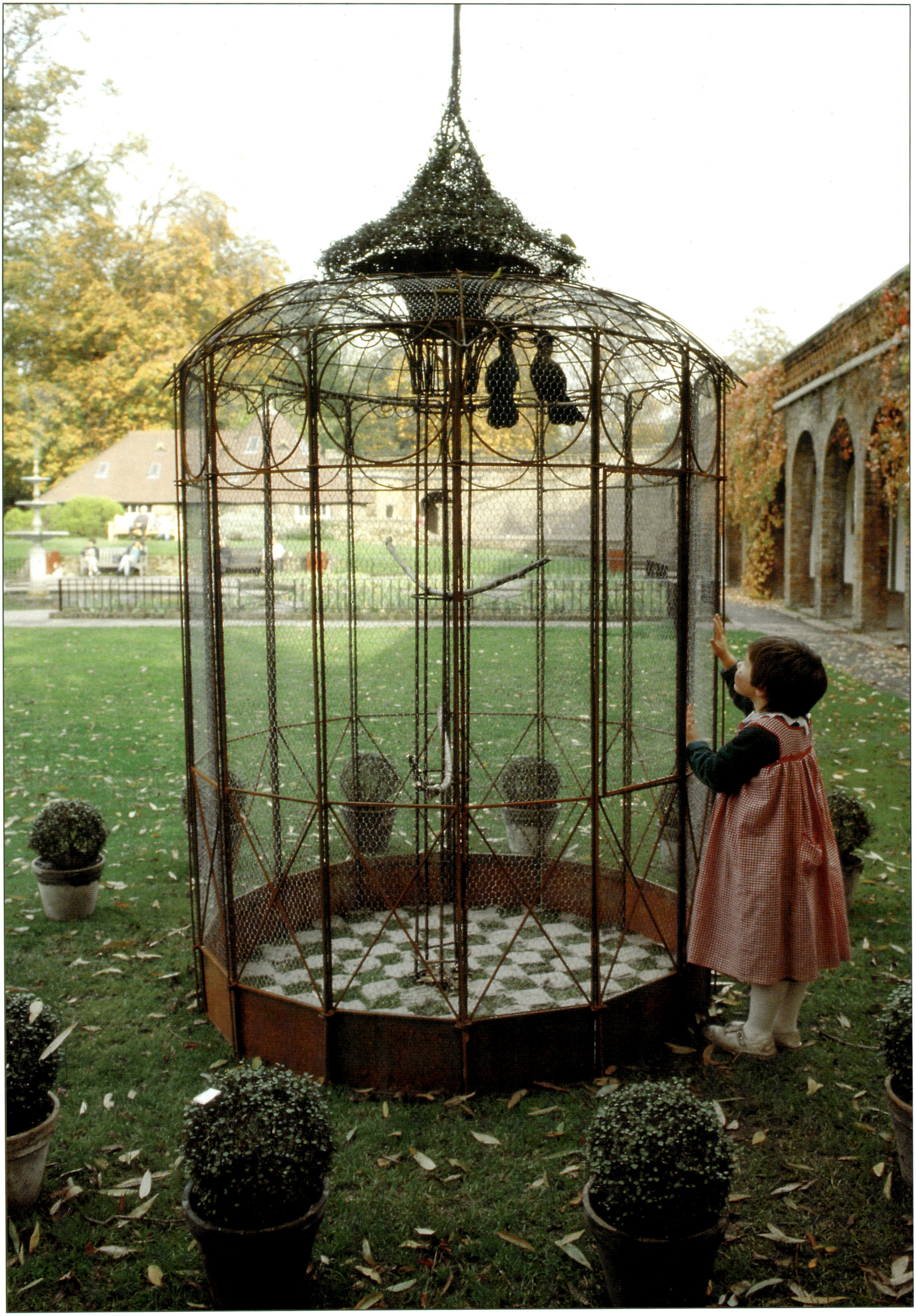

This gigantic chandelier is in a combination of iron, glass and Filipino mussel shells. The tall lily vases were created in collaboration with the glass artist Darryle Hinz.
To the left, a quite unique basket topped with a wreath of ivy leaves, all in iron, filled here with pink arum lilies.

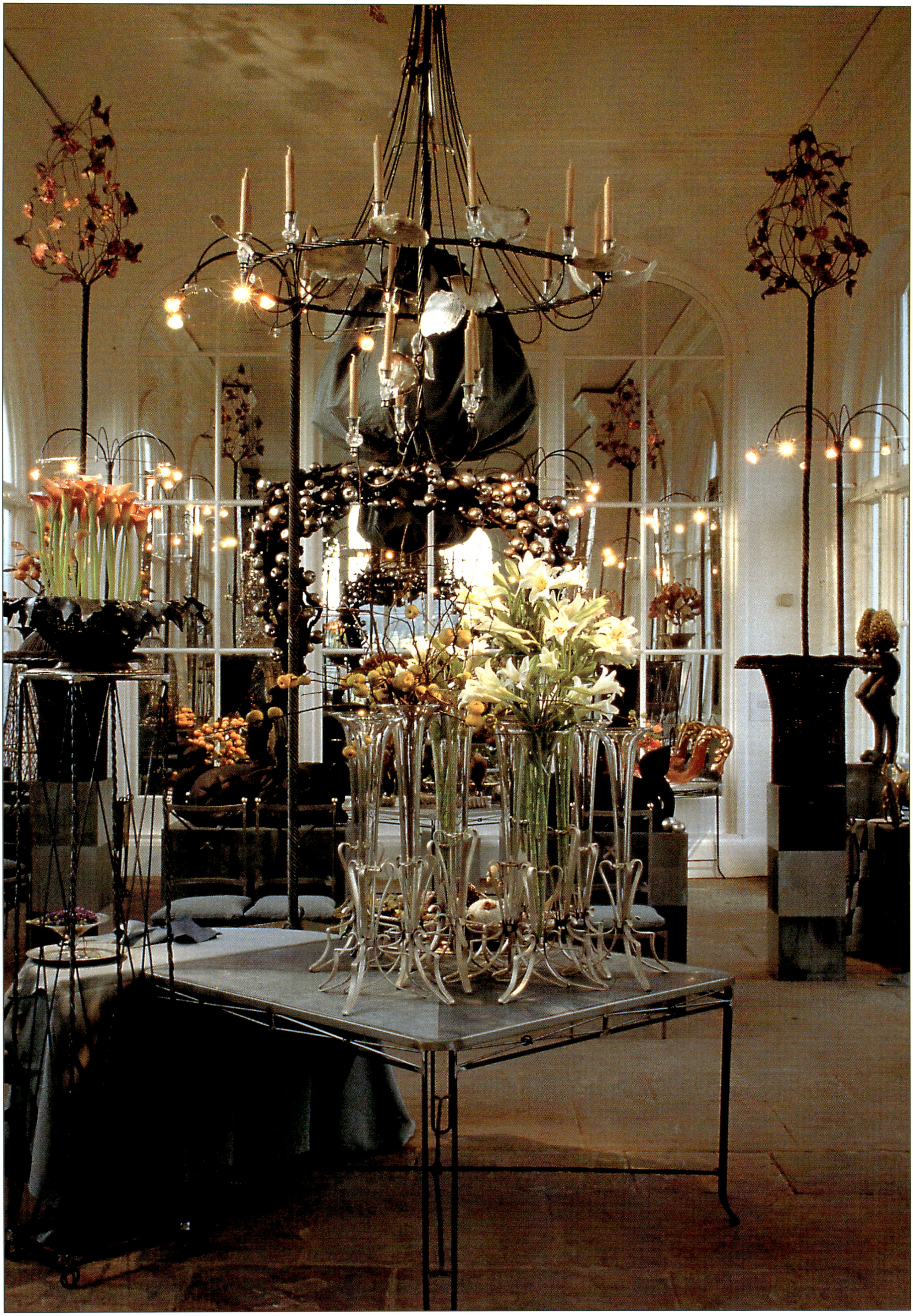

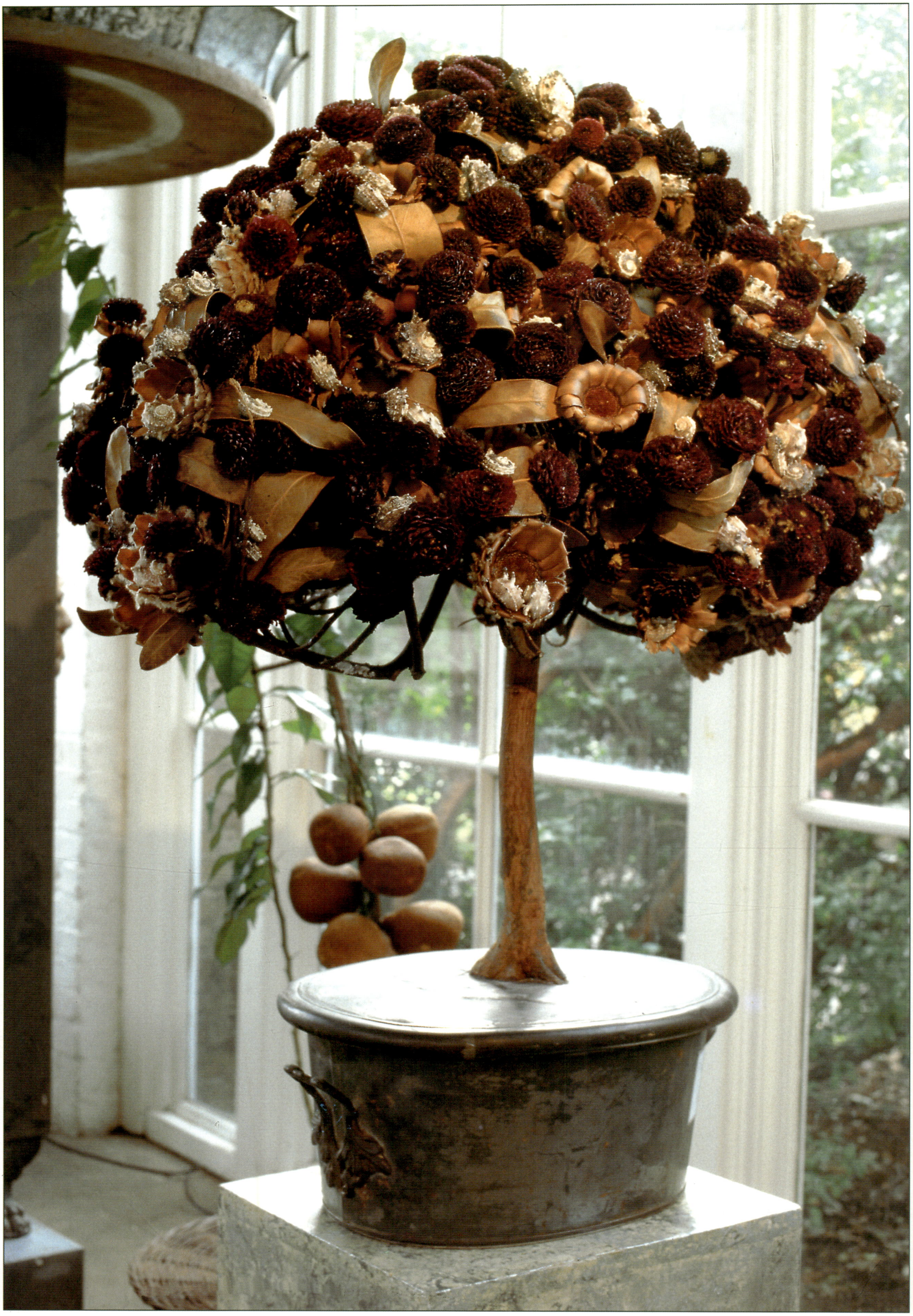

On the previous page, a quite corpulent tree made of dahlias, protea and exotic snails.
On this page can be seen an almost religious creation with rosa Osmeinsis pterasantha *and blood-red roses. In the background, 3 foot trees with preserved camellias on twisted iron stems.*

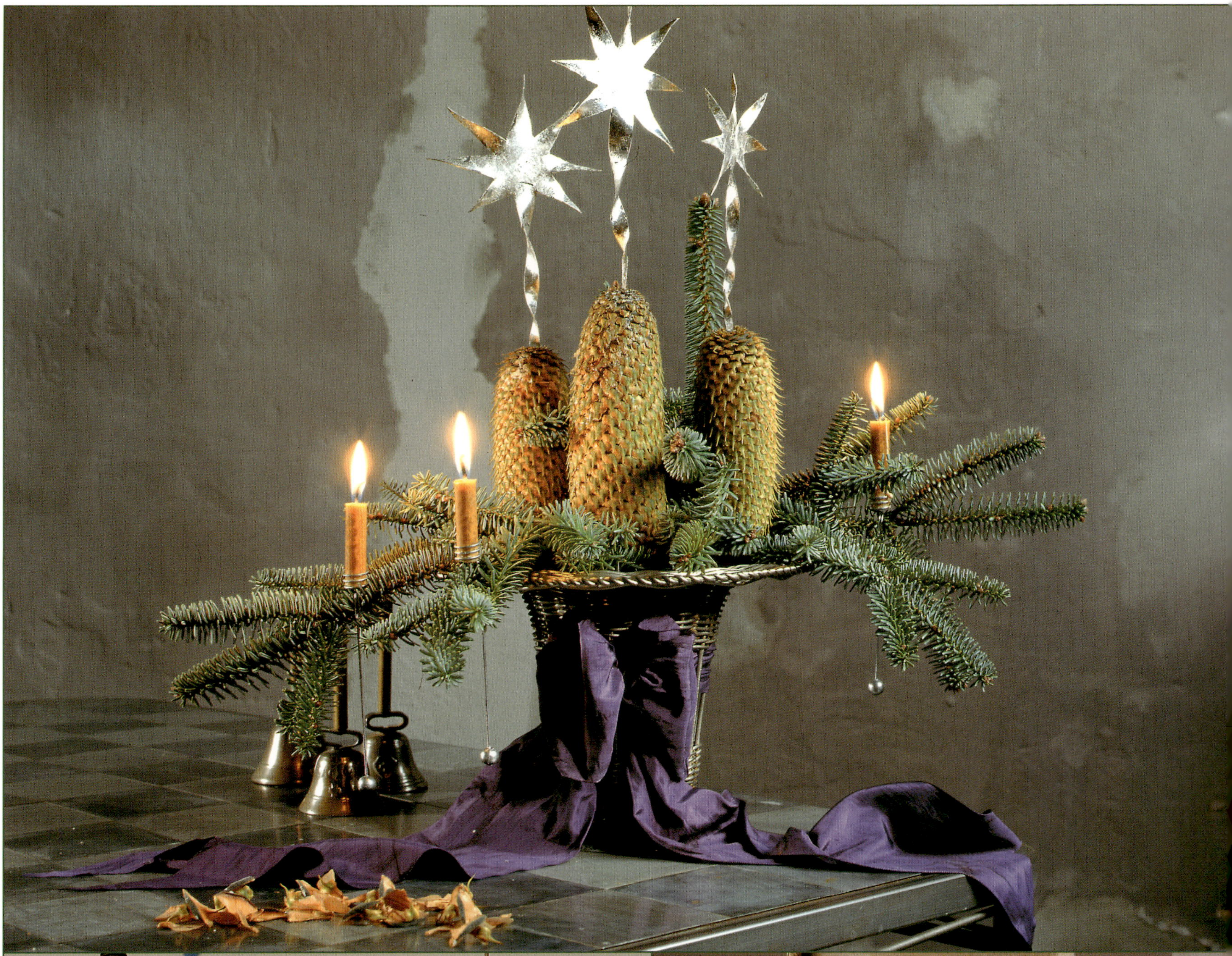
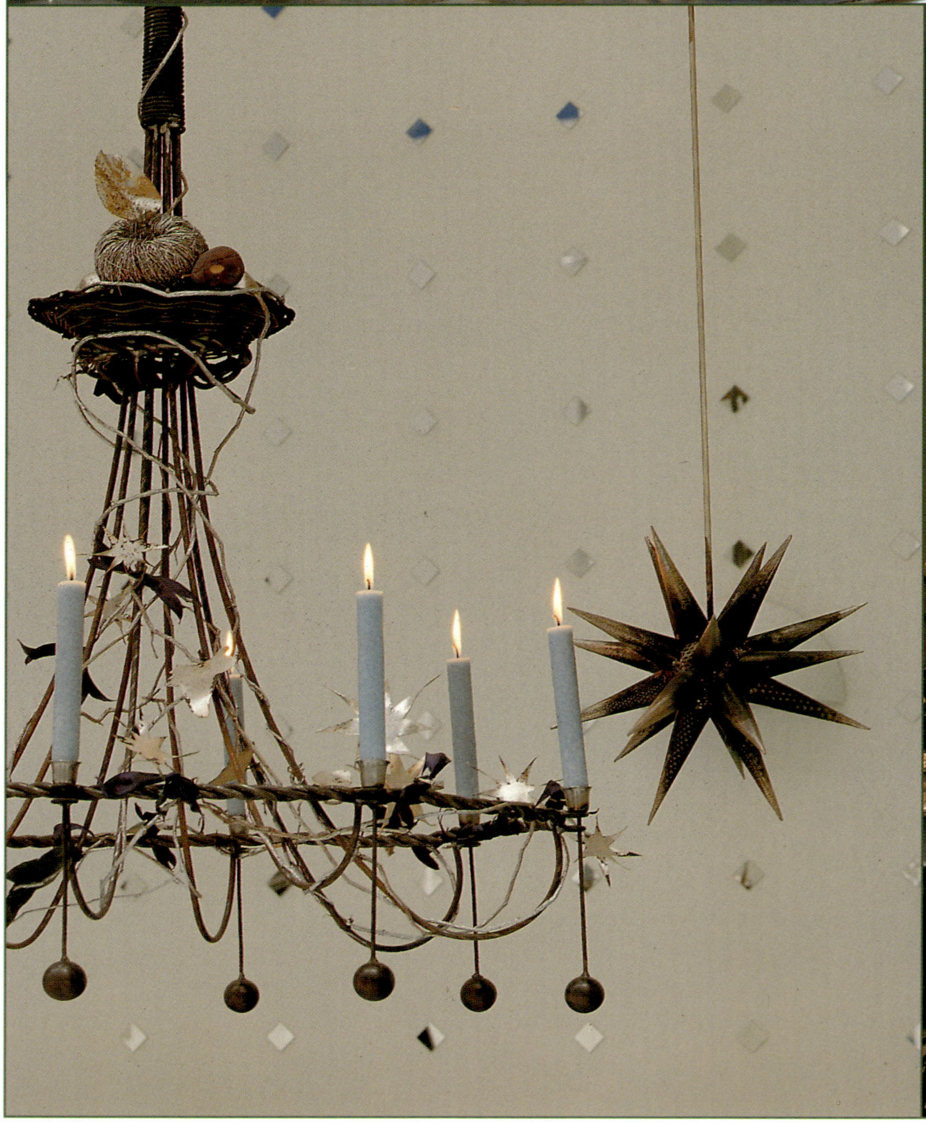
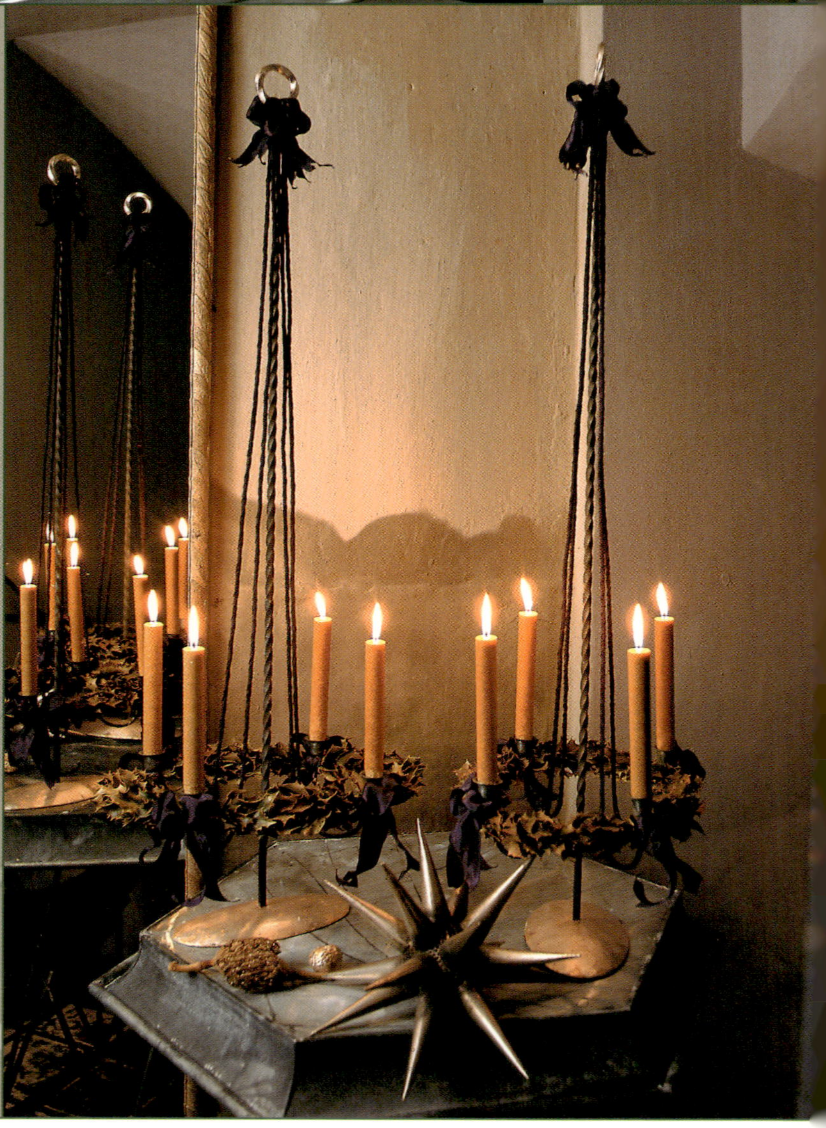

This Christmas was for me such a very starry Christmas, where the star symbol went through most of our creations. I filled a so-called vase-basket, plaited in iron with a ceramic liner, with fir and gigantic Abies nobilis *cones and stars clipped from silver-plated metal. These baskets were in a numbered series of 36. The year was 1989.*
The Empire chandelier to the left was a commission, whilst, on the other hand, the Advent wreaths are a firm tradition.

The agaves are for me a chapter in themselves and therefore they are also brought into my picture at Christmas. Here each almost competes to tell its own fairy-tale.
Star desserts made in pine-cone scales and borne on snails contain pistachio dessert covered with fondant.

Christmas 1988 was in a Byzantine glow. Somewhat unusually, we had a guest exhibitor in the building, the Italian icon-painter Mara Maccari. I sought to make our own Christmas things match the oriental. Incense and Gregorian chant filled the place.

145

The New Year table, the last festive board of the year. For this I have gathered the things I am most fond of, things that symbolize the past and the coming years, for example, purity, fertility and love and finally the crystal ball for the future.

For me, orchids are also New Year and winter.

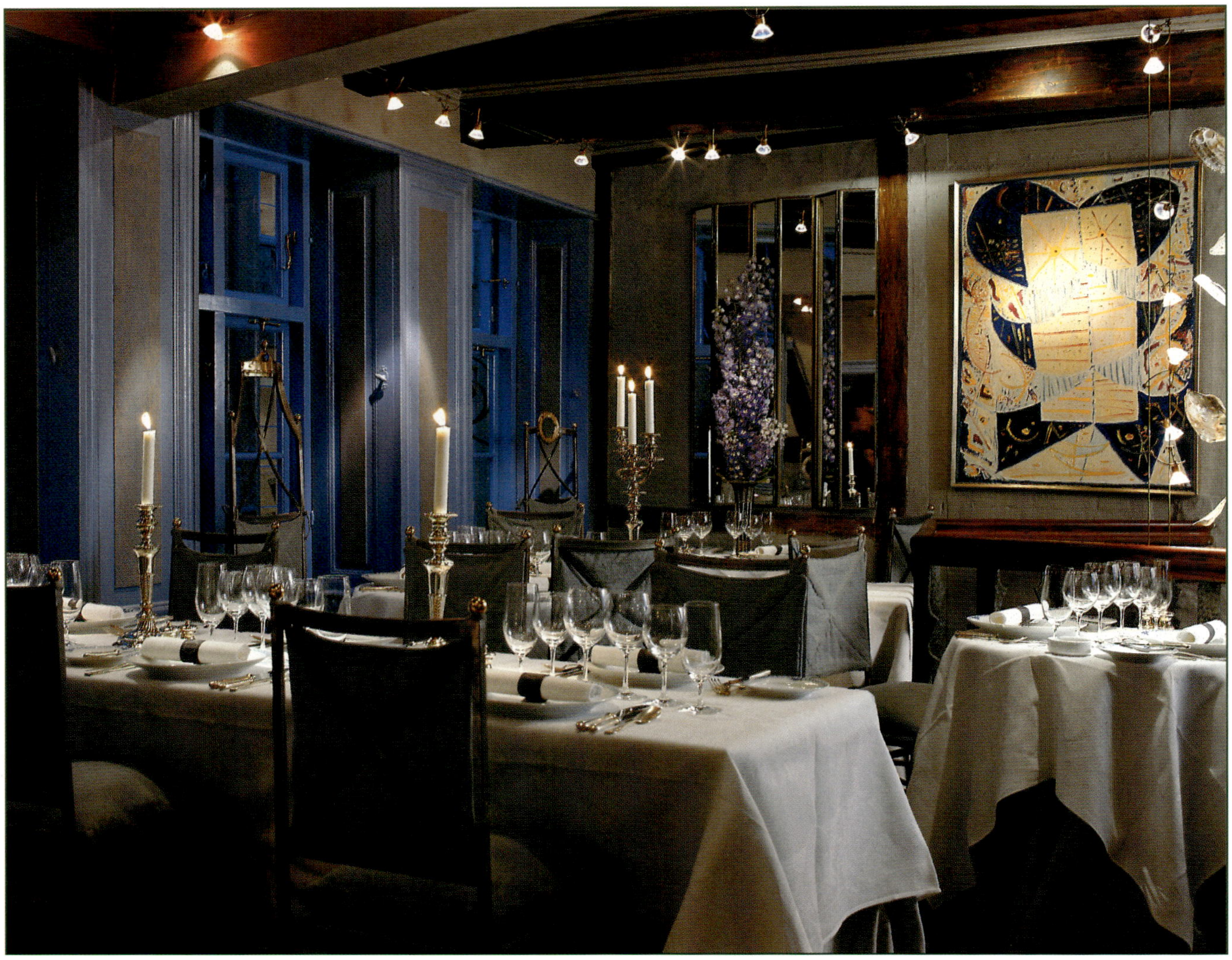

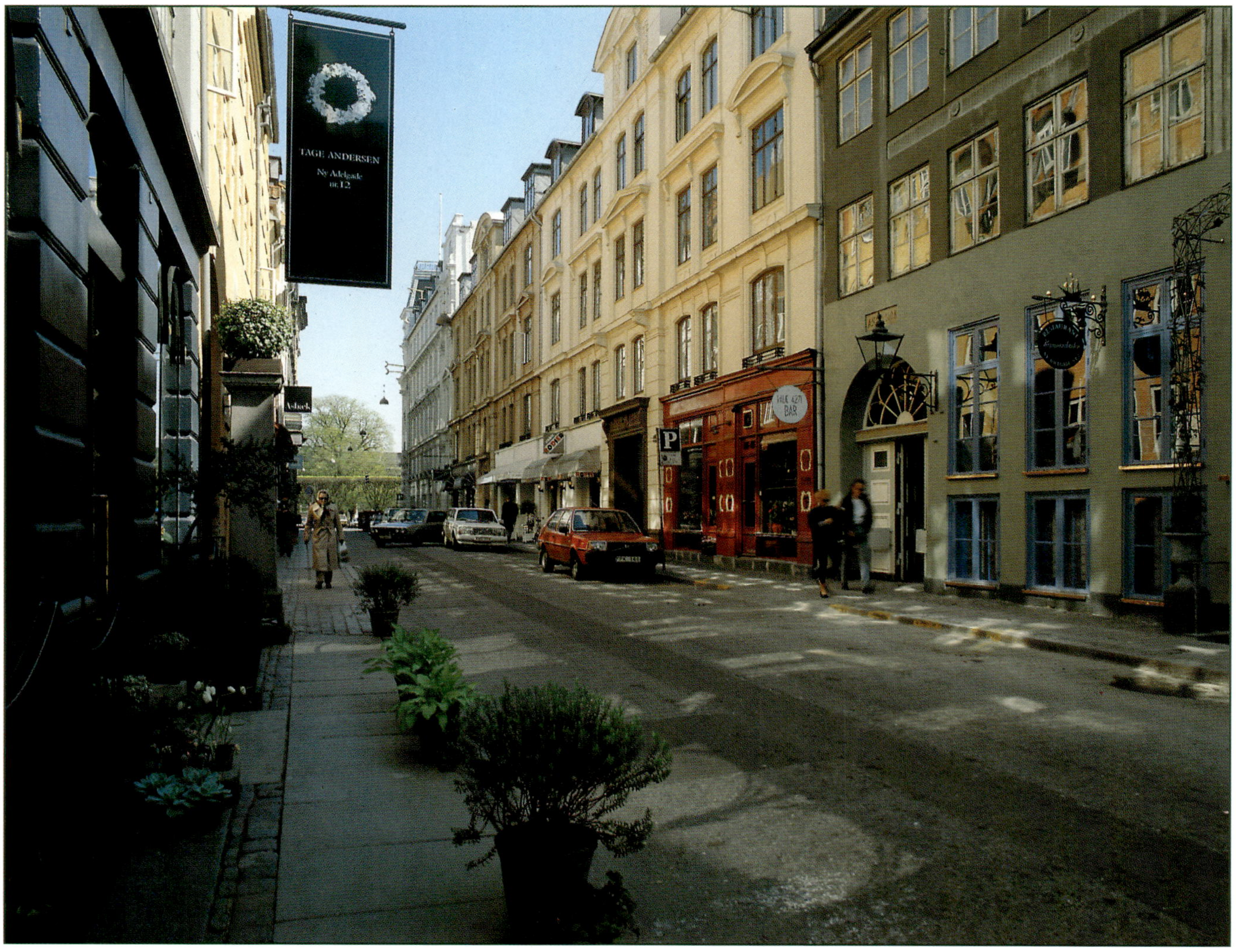
TAGE ANDERSEN
Ny Adelgade
nr.12

In 1988, I was given the task of fitting out Restaurant Kommandanten on the opposite side of Ny Adelgade. This became a brilliant pendant and an unconditional success. The restaurant has room for 52 people.

The building is from the 1700s, so we kept to materials like distemper and linseed oil with lime. The saturated colour scheme and the intimacy of the small rooms with the specially made furniture is rounded off by an exquisite kitchen.

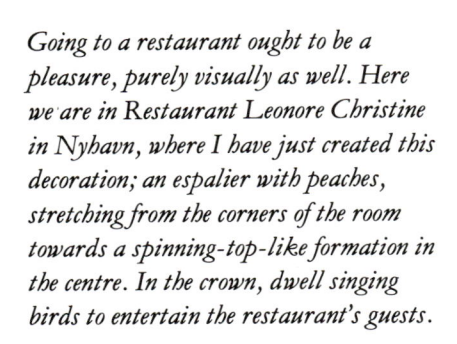

Going to a restaurant ought to be a pleasure, purely visually as well. Here we are in Restaurant Leonore Christine in Nyhavn, where I have just created this decoration; an espalier with peaches, stretching from the corners of the room towards a spinning-top-like formation in the centre. In the crown, dwell singing birds to entertain the restaurant's guests.

I fitted out Restaurant Nouvelle on Gammel Strand in Copenhagen in 1988. The light and airy atmosphere is emphasized by the glazed lemon-yellow walls. The lighting was specially made for the restaurant, the enormous chandeliers being shaped as espaliers overgrown with citrus fruits. The unique cutlery is of oxidized zinc.
In 1990, Restaurant Nouvelle was awarded a star in the Guide Michelin.

Here I have been playing for the sake of it.
Leggy garlands in antique vases compete with scented hyacinths
and oriental willow. Decoration for a fur show 1990.

Roman chariot with pumpkin – a show-piece from the Rosenborg Exhibition 1988.

Dummy peach-tree: if one is making a tree, I enjoy it when it has been made so surrealistically that it obviously is a dummy.

Étagère with preserved bird's eggs. I have made étagères in several variations to be used, for example, as fruit and cake centrepieces for buffets.

Hand-created; eggs en masse. Zinc eggs
to open and put something in. Eggs
created from fir-cone scales or ivy leaves.
Or perhaps cast in paraffin wax, light
and transparent.
Don't touch, the goose appears to say . . .

Created by hand;
sphere of oysters and conch-shells.
It is as if it is trying to come back to life . . .

The egg-concept has always preoccupied me.
So here I have developed the series in three sizes, which are made in either zinc or copper, both oxidized. Naturally, the eggs carry the stamp of the house.
On the next page I am proudly showing a tray of eggs which I made for Queen Margrethe's birthday on 16 April 1990. The tray is plaited from osiers with woodruff garlands strewed around.

This specially made monogrammed garden furniture was another birthday gift.

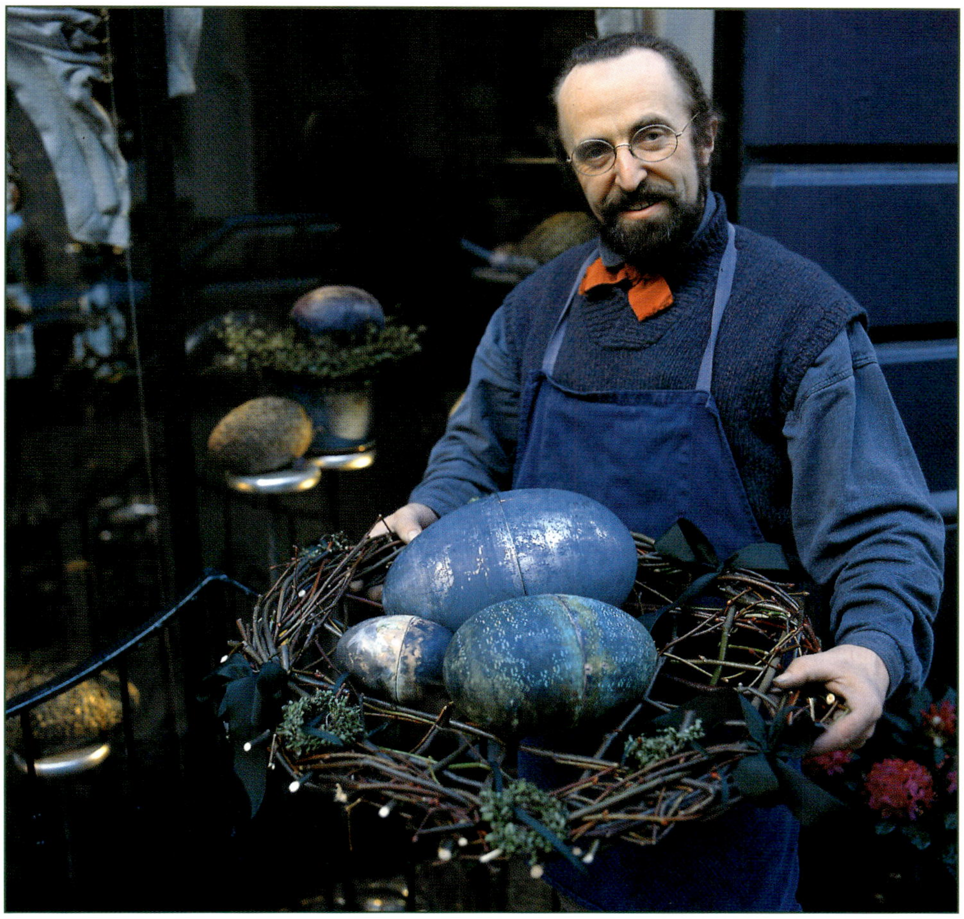

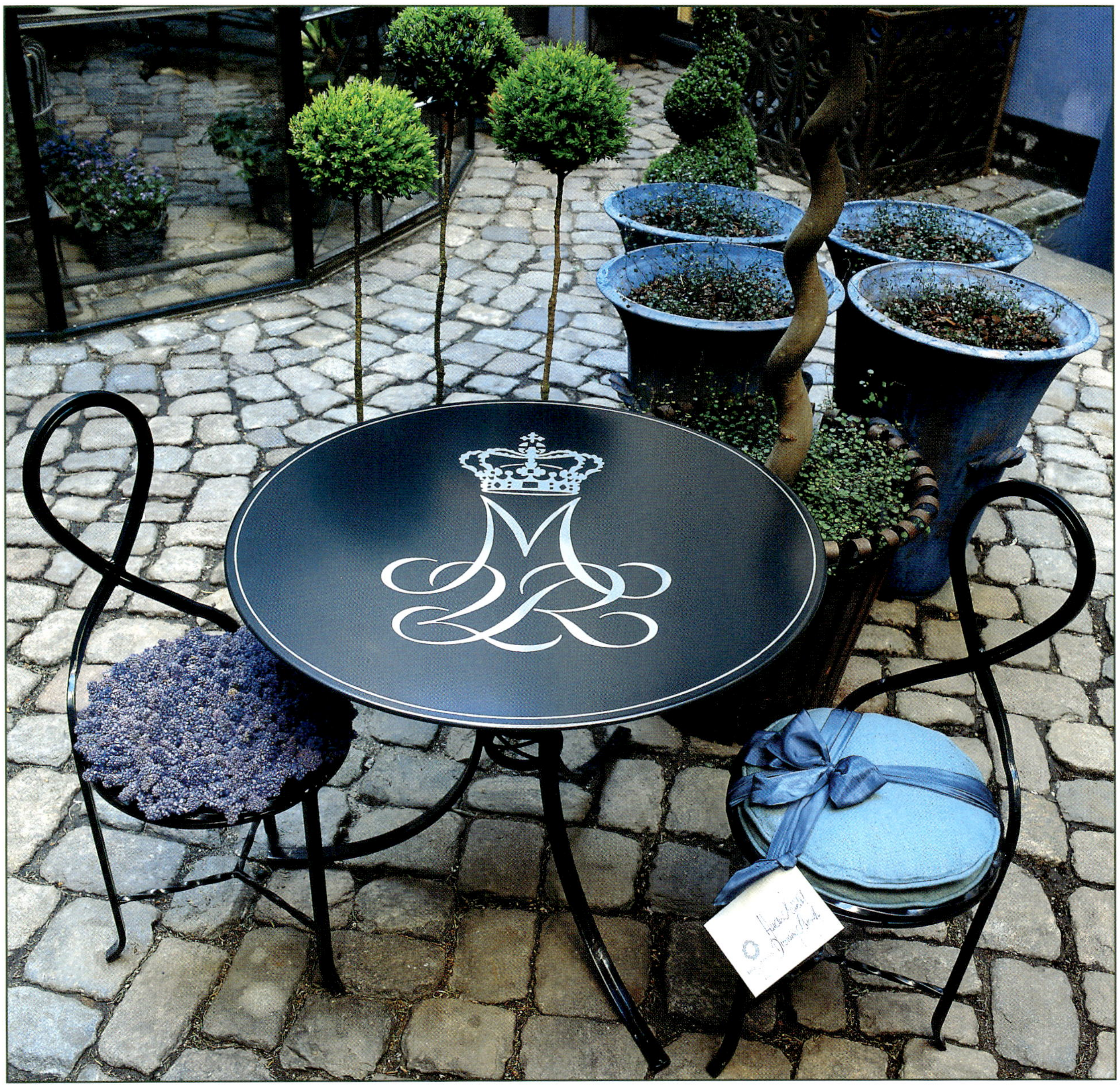

*Dinner is served . . .
And the white camellia blooms.*

On this and the following pages are shown interiors from the summer palace of Liselund, which I had the task of decorating. With the greatest respect for this 18th century house, I chose flowers which could have come from its period, here for example a »garden bouquet« of paeonies, campanulas, ground elder and delphiniums, surrounded by asters and various kinds of gypsophila.

160

161

The dining-room, probably Liselund's most characteristic room. Here I have chosen carefreeness by just placing things as they came . . . Everything is arranged in iron baskets which could have come from the Empire period. The house has often inspired me with its modest elegance so it is with enthusiasm that I carry out such a task.

The ape room, another incredible room.

*The parrot, which is only on a visit, is, in contrast to the ape, very much alive and appears to be enjoying itself.
My mission, is with small means, to bring the palace to life without it appearing decorated. So the parrot, the tray of fruit and the little sheaf with pineapples beneath are the main decorations in this room.*

Still-life. This kind of arrangement has always amused me as it makes me feel as I am in the period of the old flower-painters.
Camellia japonica »Elegance«, syngonium, banana flower, spinning top and snail-shells. 1990.

In more recent years, furniture and birdcages have taken on a larger and larger place in my repertoire. The cupboard here is one of my latest ideas. The materials are zinc, iron and glass. Six compartments, one above the other, are separated by thick glass sheets. Three of them have double doors of velvet-blue glass.

*Top: Birdcages in a row, here with
sunbirds (chinese nightingales).
Below: Composition with fruit, transferred
to film, intended as an inner window.*

*This palatial birdcage is twelve-sided
and intended for exotic birds of many kinds.
There is both air and stature, inside the cage
as well as out, for the breadth is scarcely
two metres and the height almost five metres.*

An oasis in the city. A trip through our courtyard.

*Still waters run deep. Here with goldfish
and a cover of plaited osiers.*

View from the courtyard with night illuminations.

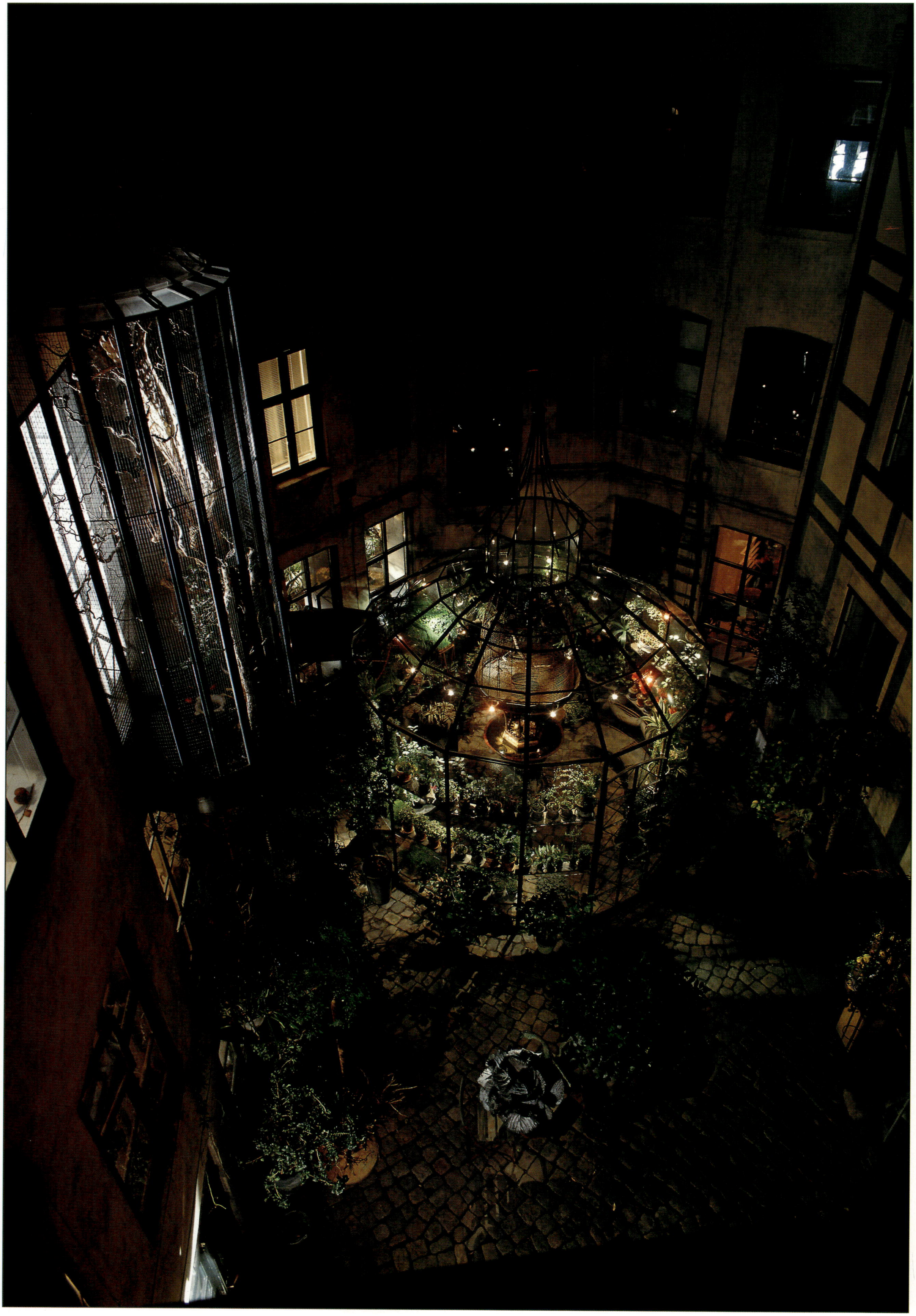

My building, – my shop, is so often compared with Aladdin's cave and other fantastic places. The following pages provide a peep into my very private world. From my balcony at the very top of the building – where the twittering of the birds competes with the stillness – I can follow the changing scenery of the courtyard (the photo on the opposite page).
Here I wish for no comparison. Here I am myself – when for a change I give myself time.
This dramatic picture is characteristic in an excellent way of the atmosphere on the following pages.
Pages 172-173: the living-room with a peep into my workroom.
Pages 174-175: The kitchen where the whole building meets for morning coffee at eight o'clock every day.

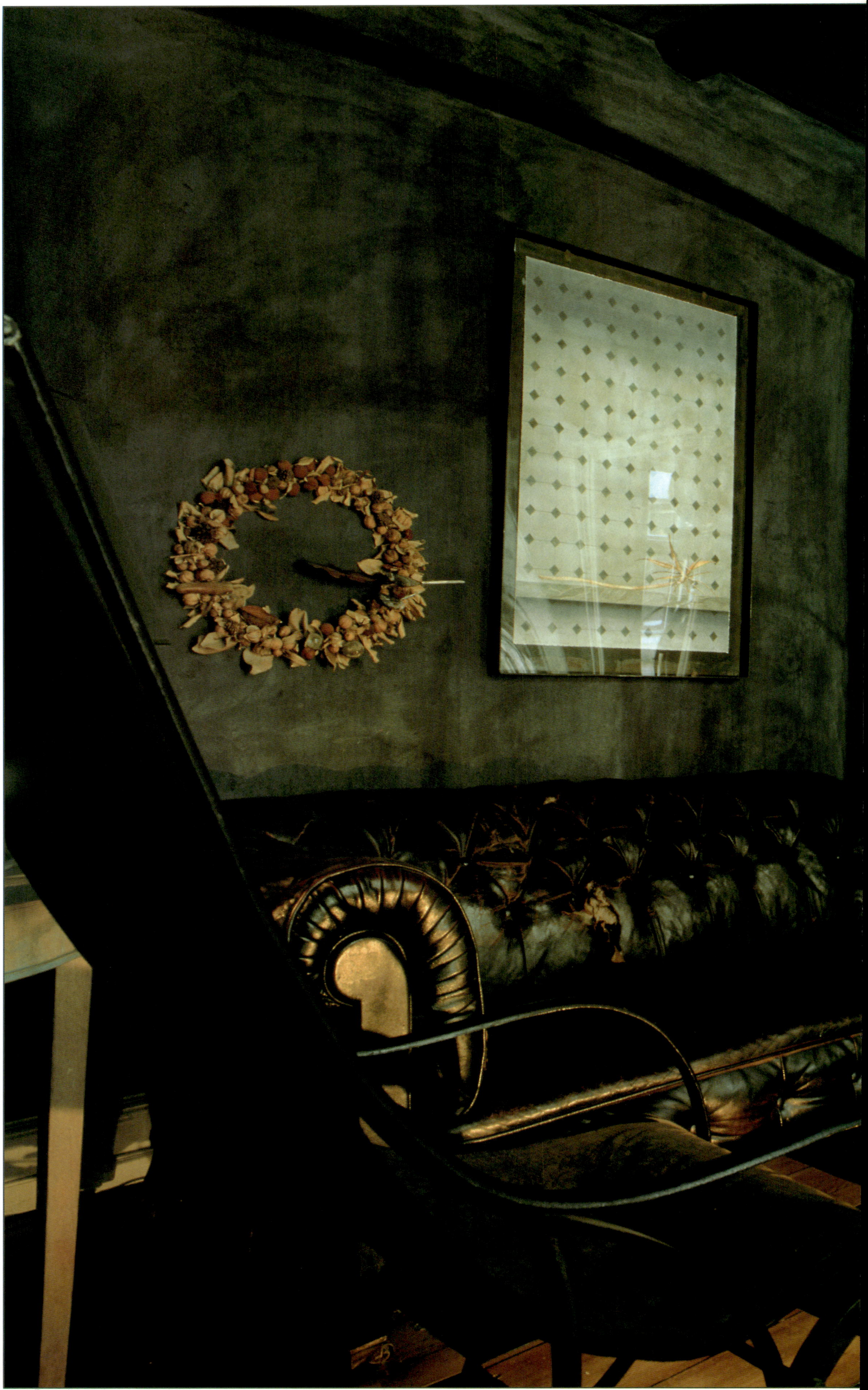

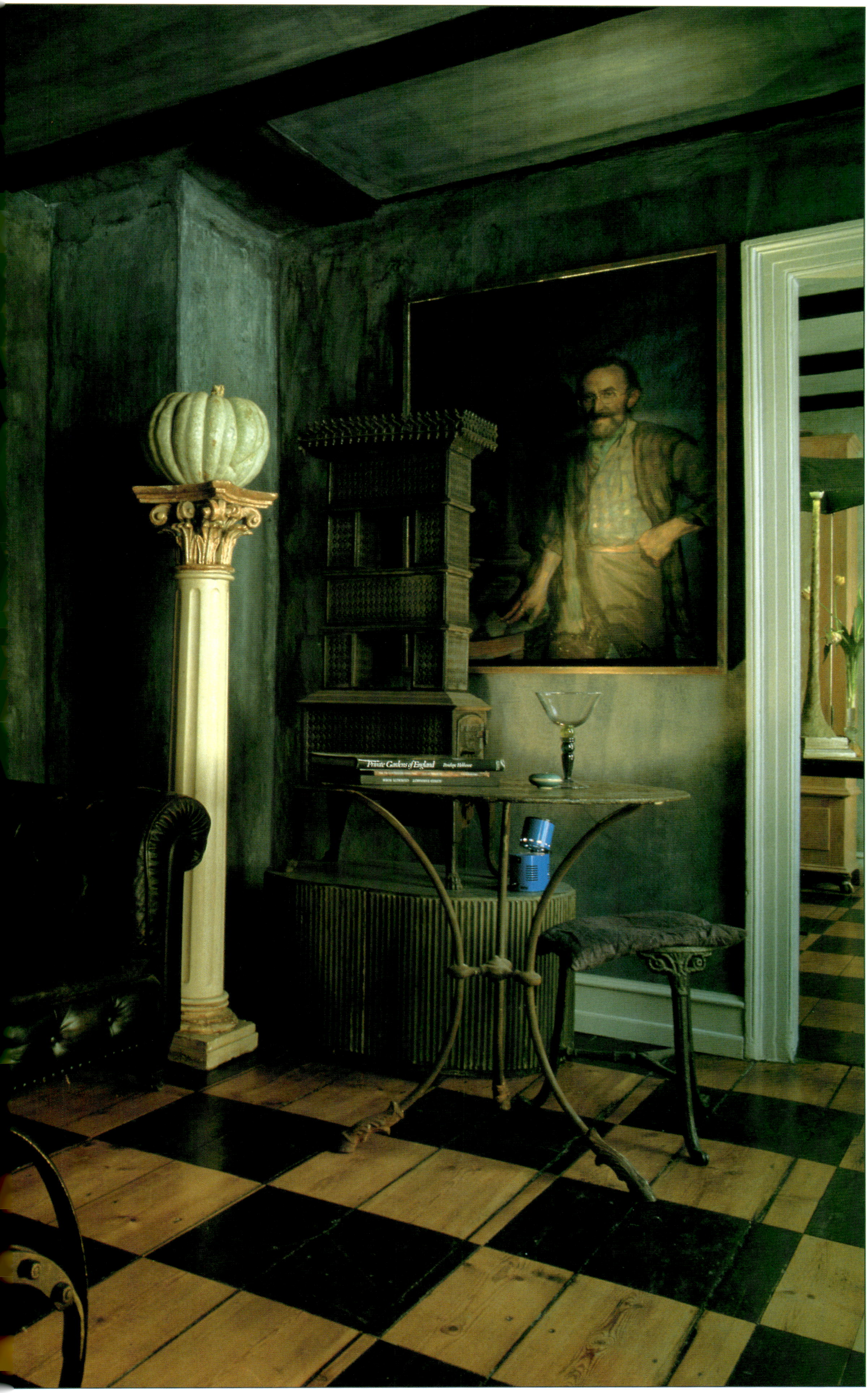
Private Gardens of England

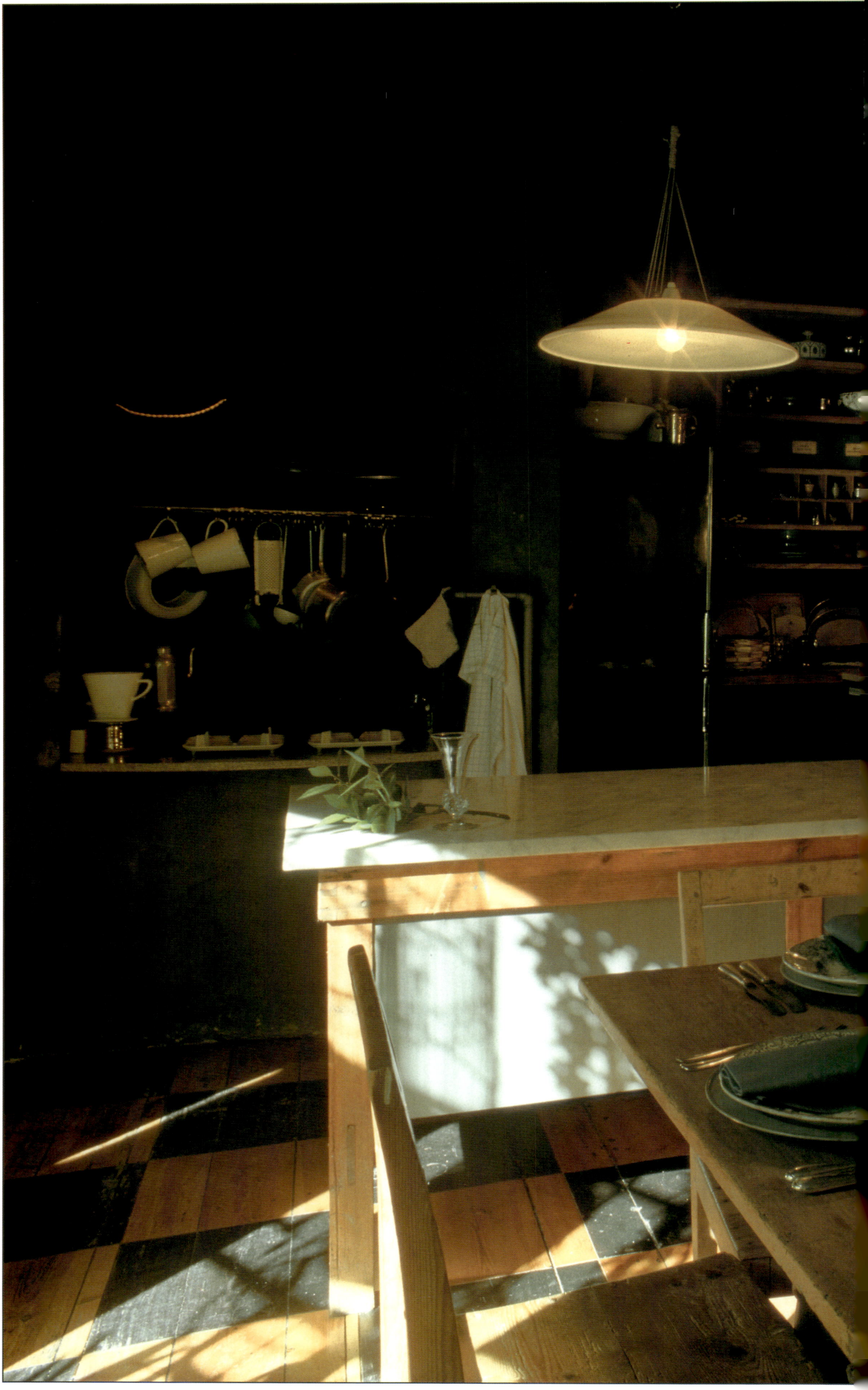

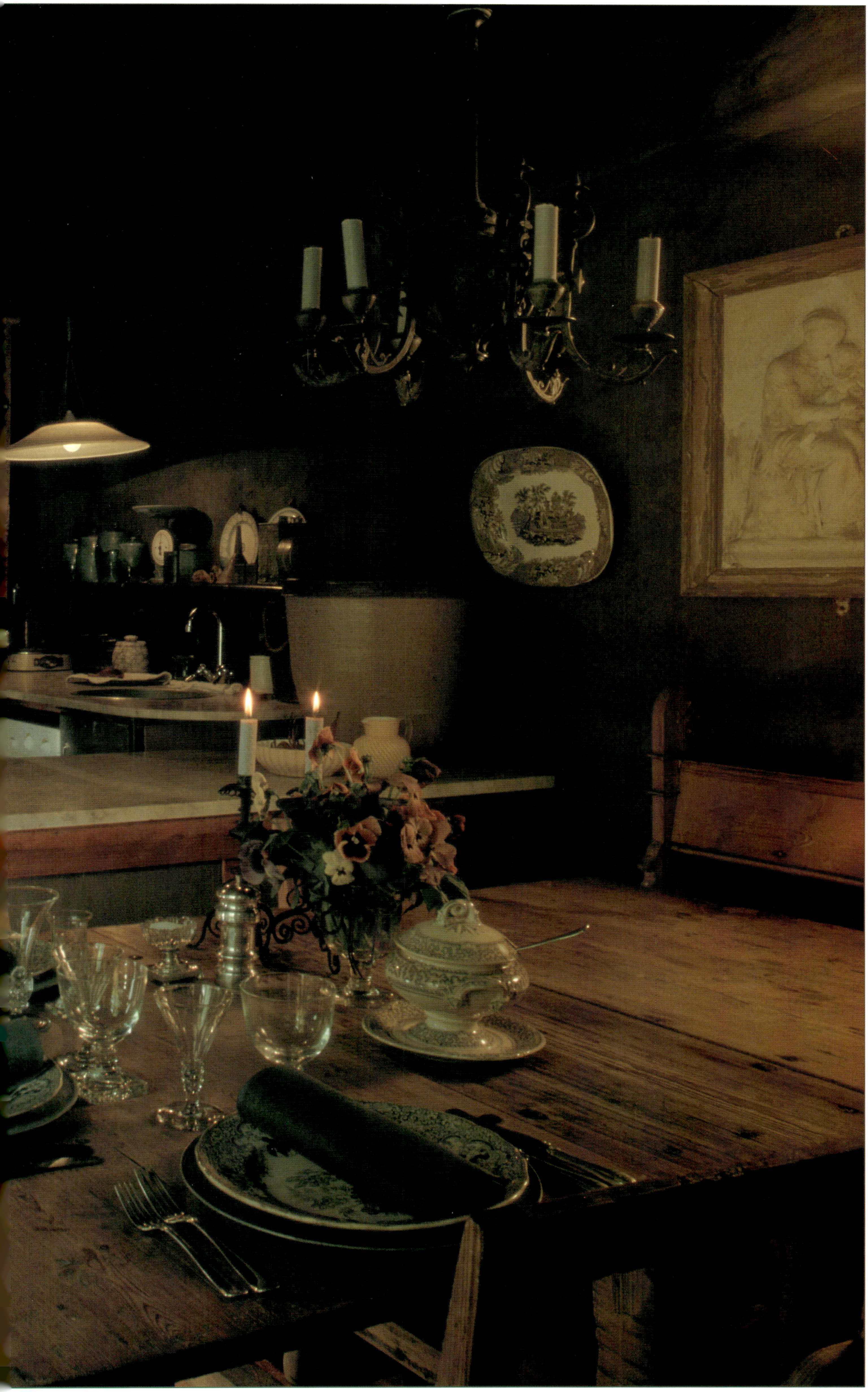

*The pig lives permanently on the kitchen
table and appears to enjoy its own radiance.*

*From the kitchen one goes up a floor to
a combinerd drawing-room and bedroom.*

*Despite the almost coke-grey wall colour,
the most incredible light can get into the kitchen.*

176

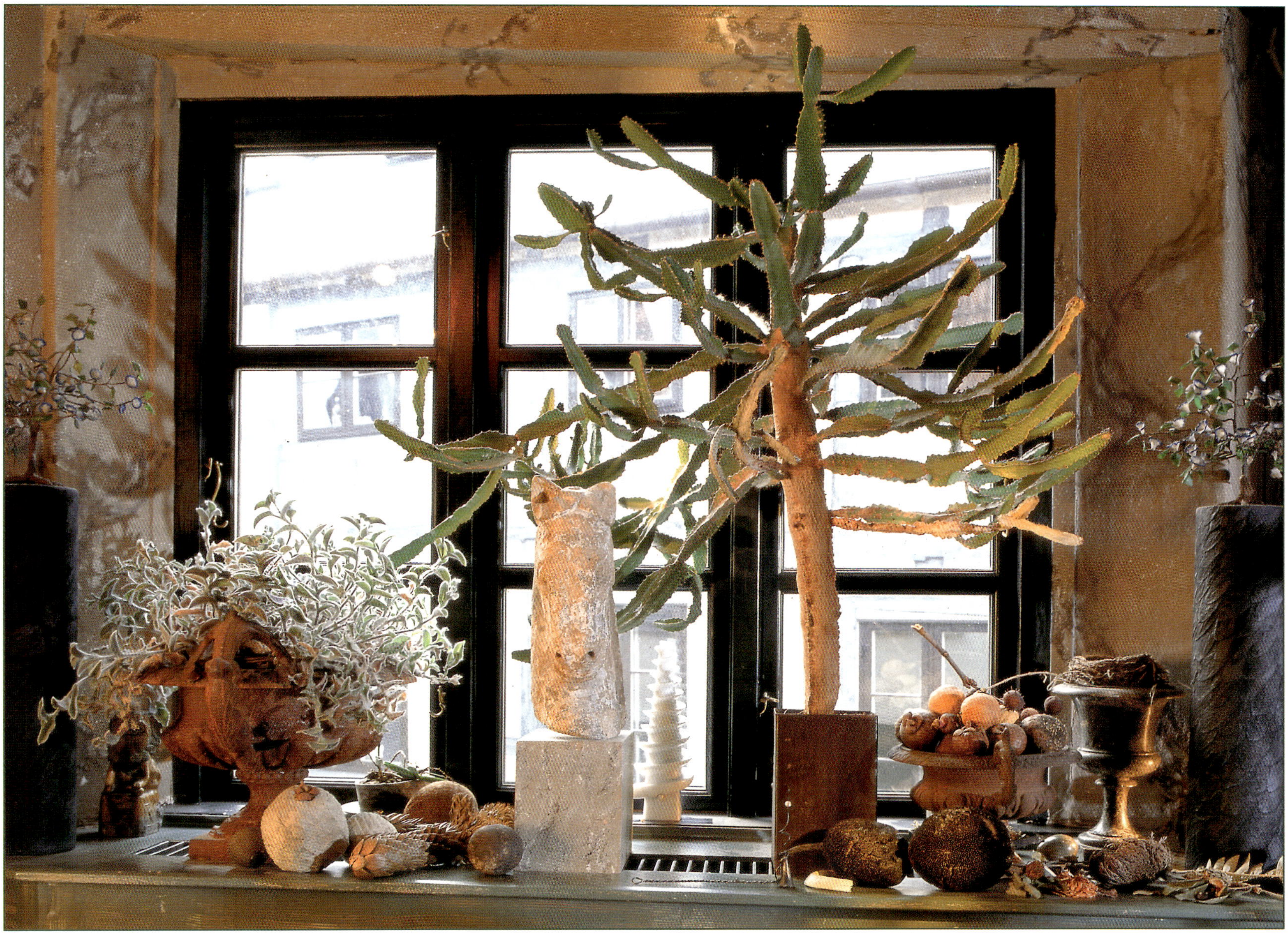

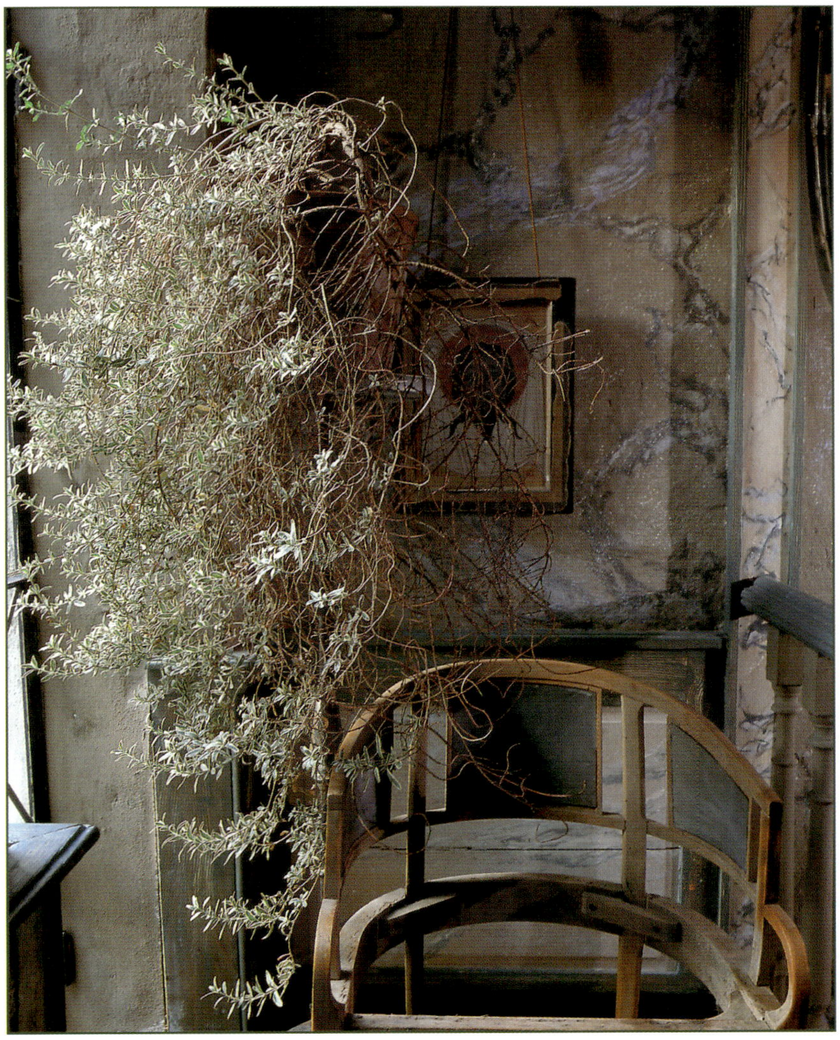

In the drawing-room I have kept to earth colours and have let innumerable marblings mark in the space. In my private existence, I like unobtrusiveness and surround myself mainly with things I have been given throughout the years.

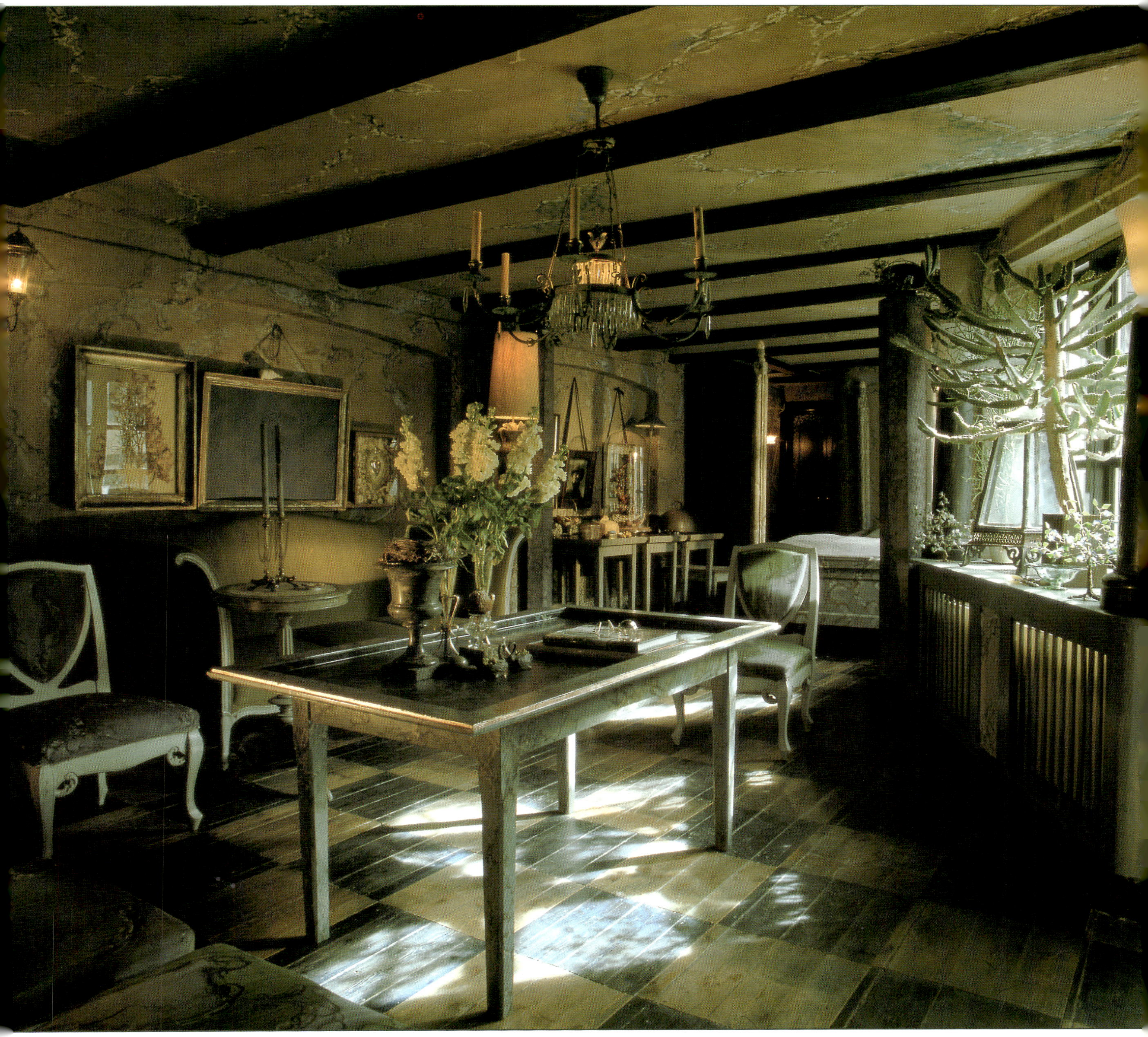

The bathroom.
Floor in metal squares, zinc and copper.
Walls clad to panel height in zinc.

*The squares from the floor are allowed
to mirror themselves in the outer side of the bath.
Screens at the windows in a combination of
mirror and matt glass make curtains superfluous.*

182

*Three independent arrangements where I have
placed the weight upon the dramatic and the sculptural.
I. Scabiosa seed-heads.
II. Dead muehlenbeckia plant dressed up with cattleya orchids.
III. Pepper-root leaves with snails.*

*The photographer's skill emphasizes, no,
rather creates the drama in this instant.
The trees are made of protea inflorescences and mussels.*

Banksia inflorescences in a dramatic setting, flanked by Lynn Chadwick sculptures.

Interior: arrangement in our own building. Here too the so often utilized floors. The high-backed chair is a unique one.
At the work-table, I feel that it also brings peace to the soul to be surrounded by beautiful things one likes.

Another unique chair. The marbled table has a sunken plate in enamelled iron.
The bouquet is autumn and a composition very typical of me; many different sorts of chrysanthemum, French anemones and protea.

I have had much pleasure in the juxtaposition of copper and zinc. Here partly floor-covering, partly café tables.

Another example of a chequered console. We plait the vase baskets in iron wire which is nickel-plated. Here with a zinc liner. Scales from Abies nobilis *cones have here become trees.*

Modelled pot with ivy and doves.

Left: Cake made of leaves, photographed against a mural in café style painted by Robert Cullen.

Right: Arrangement against a mural, with rudbeckia seed-heads set up in the form of a sphere.

Above: arrangement from the shop. Zinc egg in holder, here in gold-leaf, in which hyacinths can be cultivated, as shown. The bulb rests on an inset grid so that the roots can reach the water in the bottom of the egg.
To the right: a tumbler, sweet corn in a copper bowl.

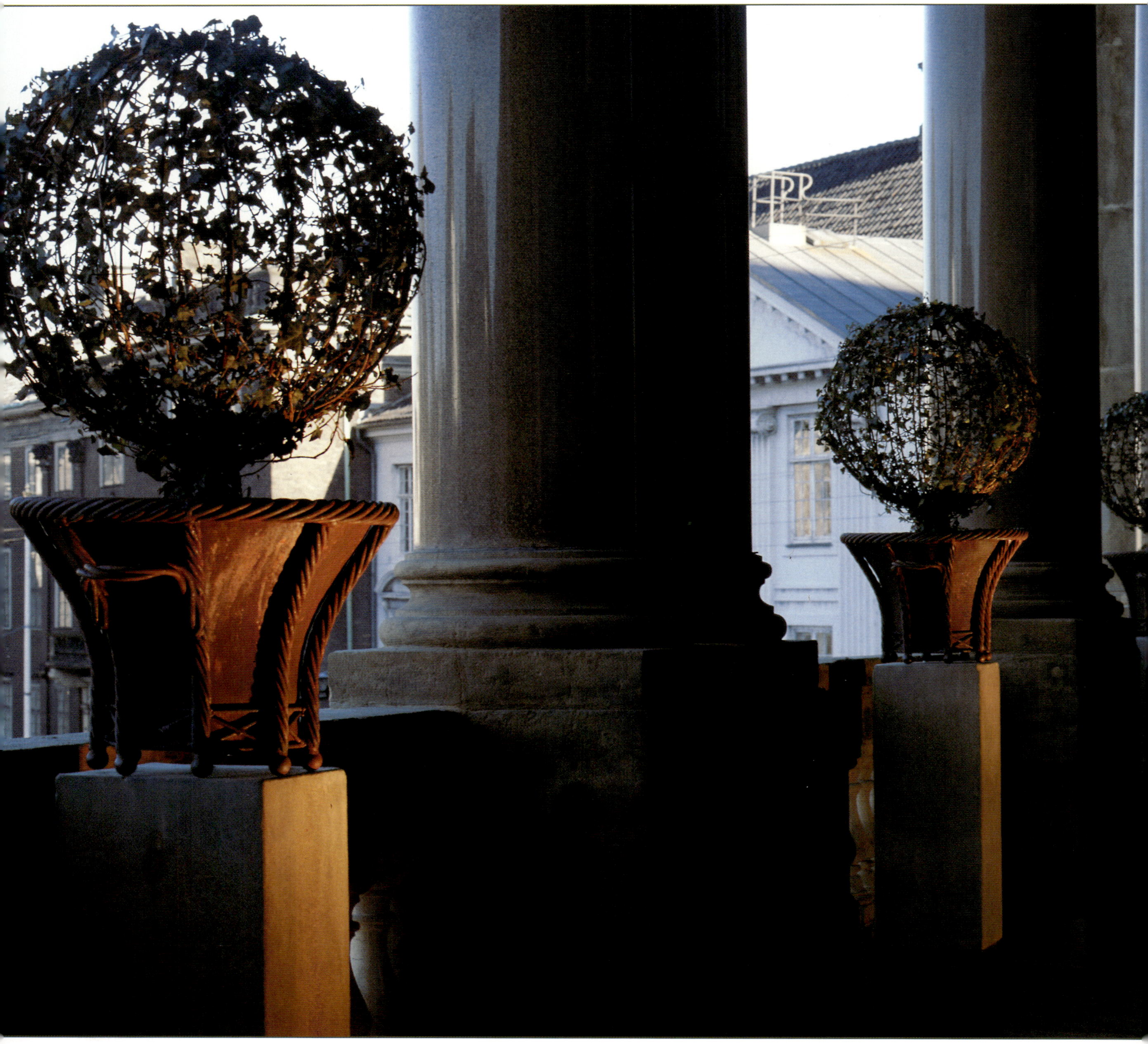

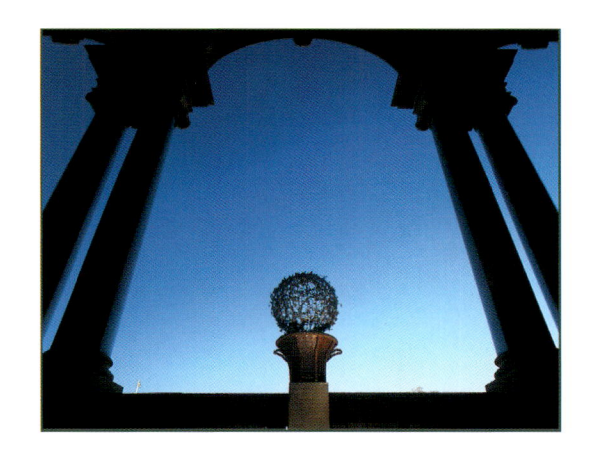

Stationary decoration on the Royal Theatre's balcony on to Kongens Nytorv in Copenhagen.
Vases and constructions for the ivy balls are worked in iron, the diameter being 80 cm.
Below: clipped muehlenbeckia, also on espaliers of iron wire.

Trees, naturalistic or abstract – the possibilities are endless. Notice the chequered pattern of the crown. Every single square consists of hundreds of scales from Abies nobilis *cones. With such a simple shape, one has to stress the importance of the interplay between crown, trunk and vase.*

Below, as on the next page, trees, seed capsules and Cobaea scandens *flowers placed on the trunk of a bourgainvillea.*

An orgy of patterns. Vase on a pillar, the Royal Theatre's balcony.

Arrangement with Cobaea scandens *trees intended as stage setting.*

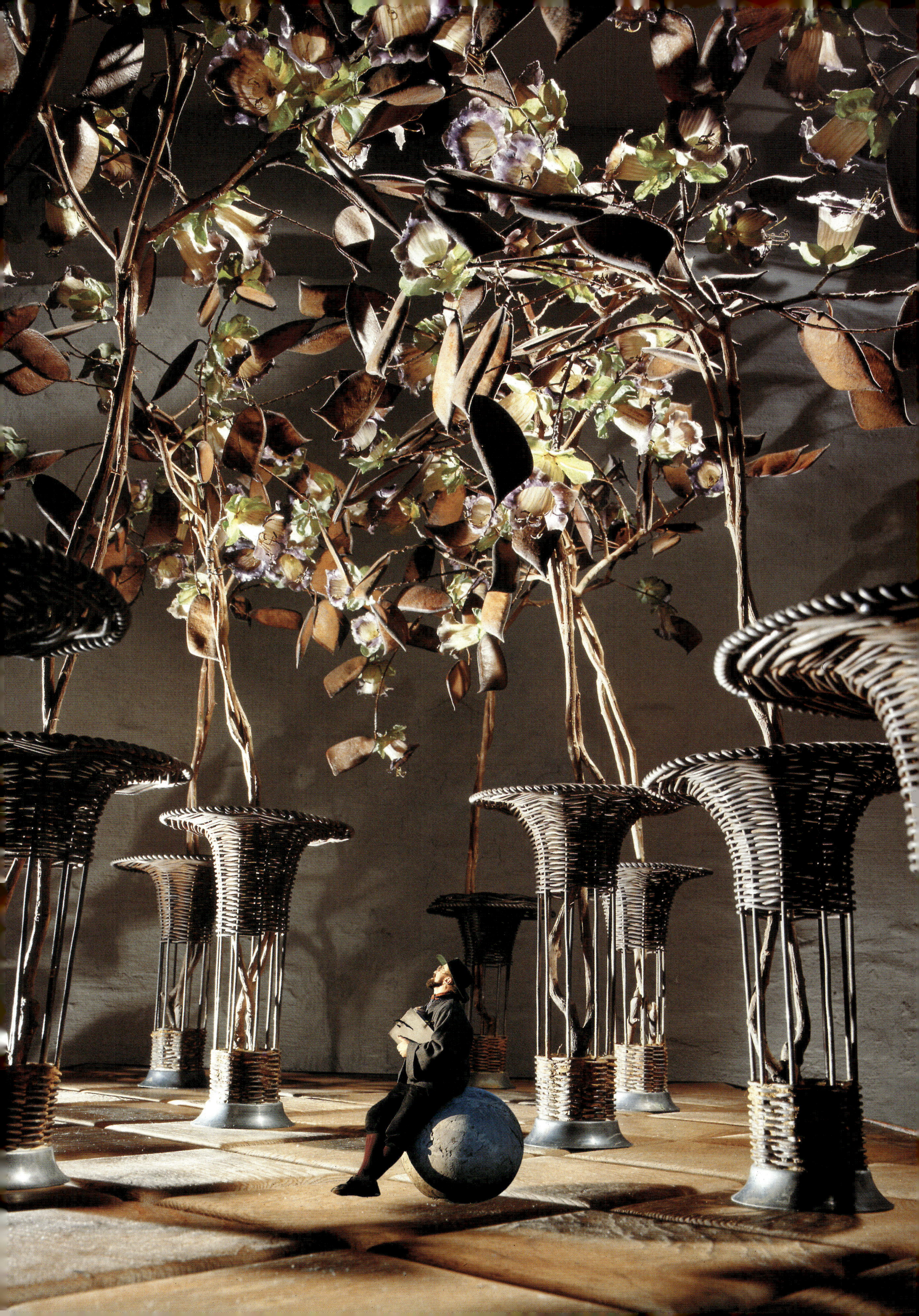

1990. My debut as a stage designer is in the Herman Bang play Intermission, *dramatized and produced by Flemming Behrendt. Erik Mørk has the role of Herman Bang.*
The performance takes place at the New Theatre in Copenhagen, where we have created a small, intimate theatre in a ballet rehearsal room with seats for about a hundred people.

The producer Flemming Behrendt writes of this stage set:
»On a fine day, Tage Andersen's version of the decadent furniture appeared. It was so big that it seemed to burst the bounds of the fragile scenery. But then we discovered what it was that Tage wanted: to extend the inner world of Bang into a large theatrical symbol which the Freudians might call a womb.«

Bang's period was the Victorian age. In the setting, I tried to create an atmosphere which had its roots in that age but would also appeal to the present — and the future. The furniture is made of iron, the yellow set above with a view to resemble wood.

Arrangement of decorative elements.
With lighting, I often try not only to create a lamp but also to make it an integral part of the decoration. Here for Restaurant Petri-Pumpa in Lund, Sweden.

*Reading lamp – is what I call this
invention from Christmas 1990.*

*Chandelier with glass light-pipes and
Filipino mussel-shells, 1988.*

*The cockerels on these pages were invented as portents of New Year 1990-91. They very quickly awakened the public's enthusiasm and have already multiplied somewhat.
They are made on an armature of iron wire covered with lichen from larches. The shape is hollow so that one perceives the light through it.*

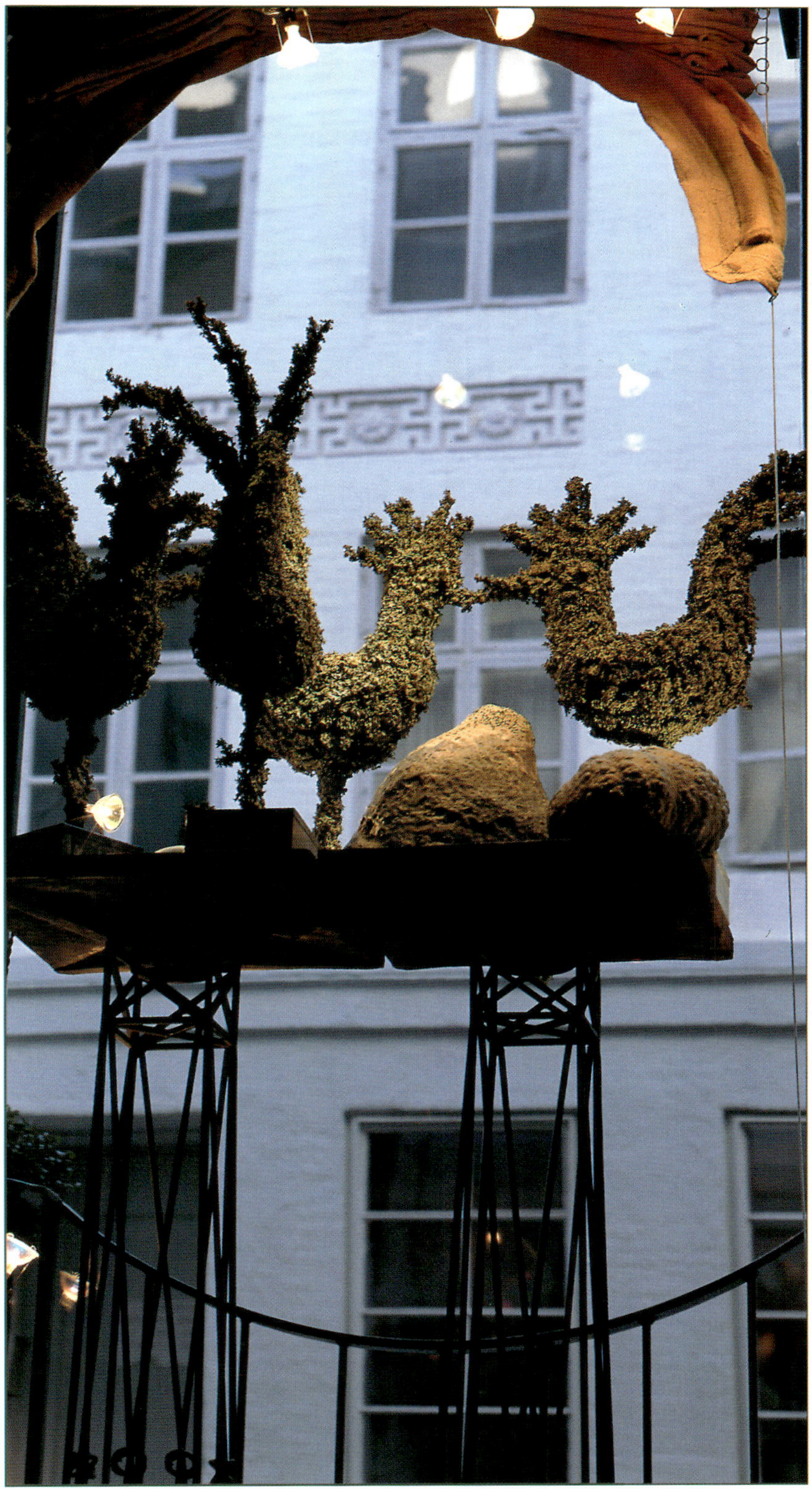

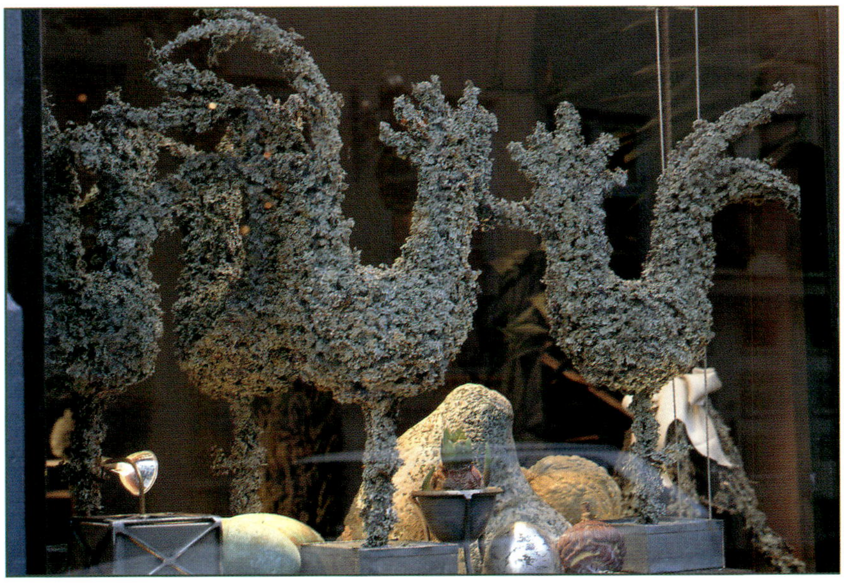

View from the garden room. When one lives in a fairy-tale, one accepts that the place for cups gets smaller. The glass table was specially made for the room.

*On pages 206 to 219 I present a house
which is a world in itself.
Once upon a time, as in so many
fairy-tales, I was asked for my assistance
upon the choice of colour for a room that
was then dark and dank. The ideas
developed and before long the room had
received this large window and door area.
With this, the foundation was laid, and
the true decoration could begin.
The room is now light and friendly,
having almost hall-like qualities. Those
who live in the house have chosen
fairy-tale and are in possession of that
grain of madness which makes life
interesting.*

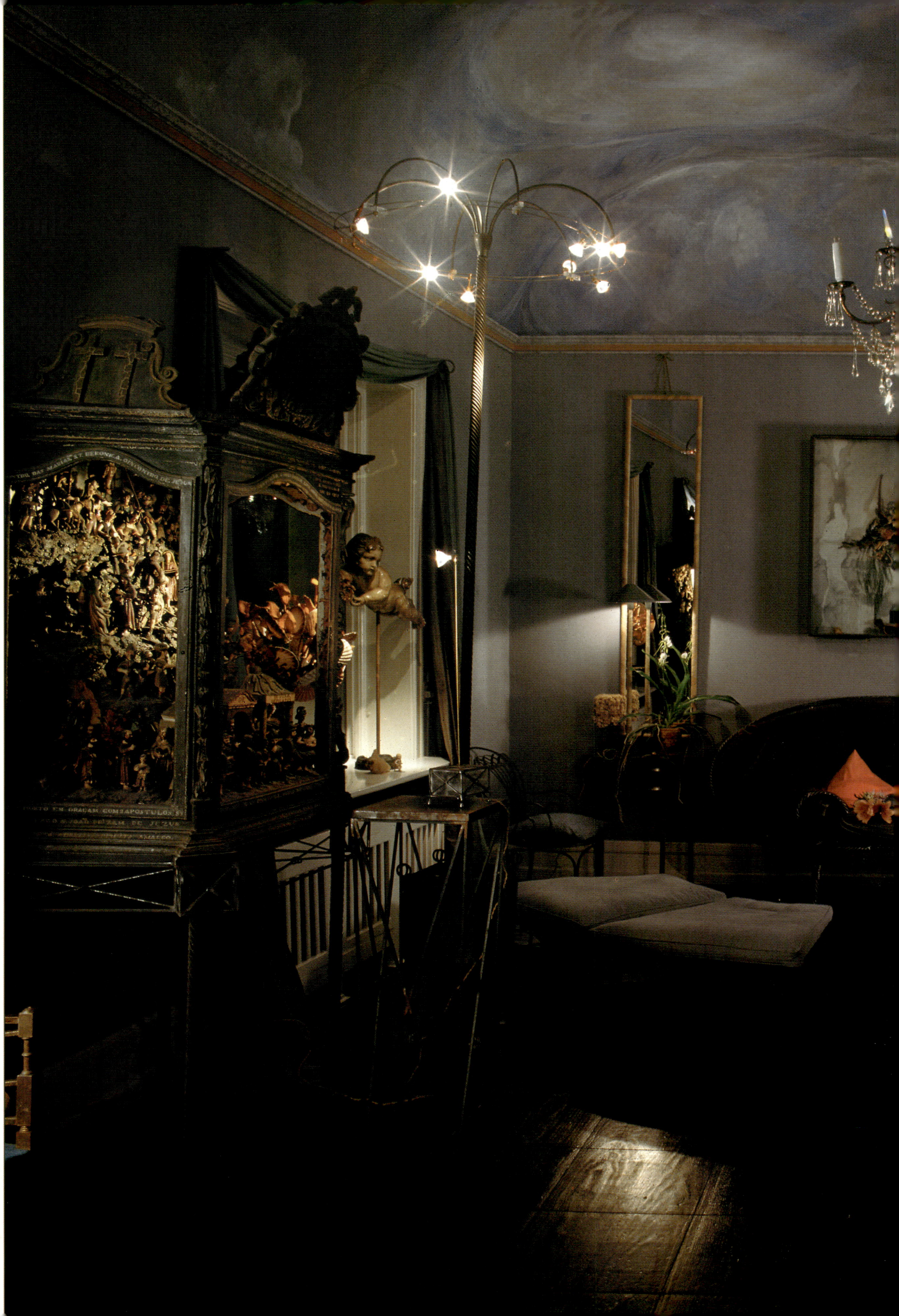

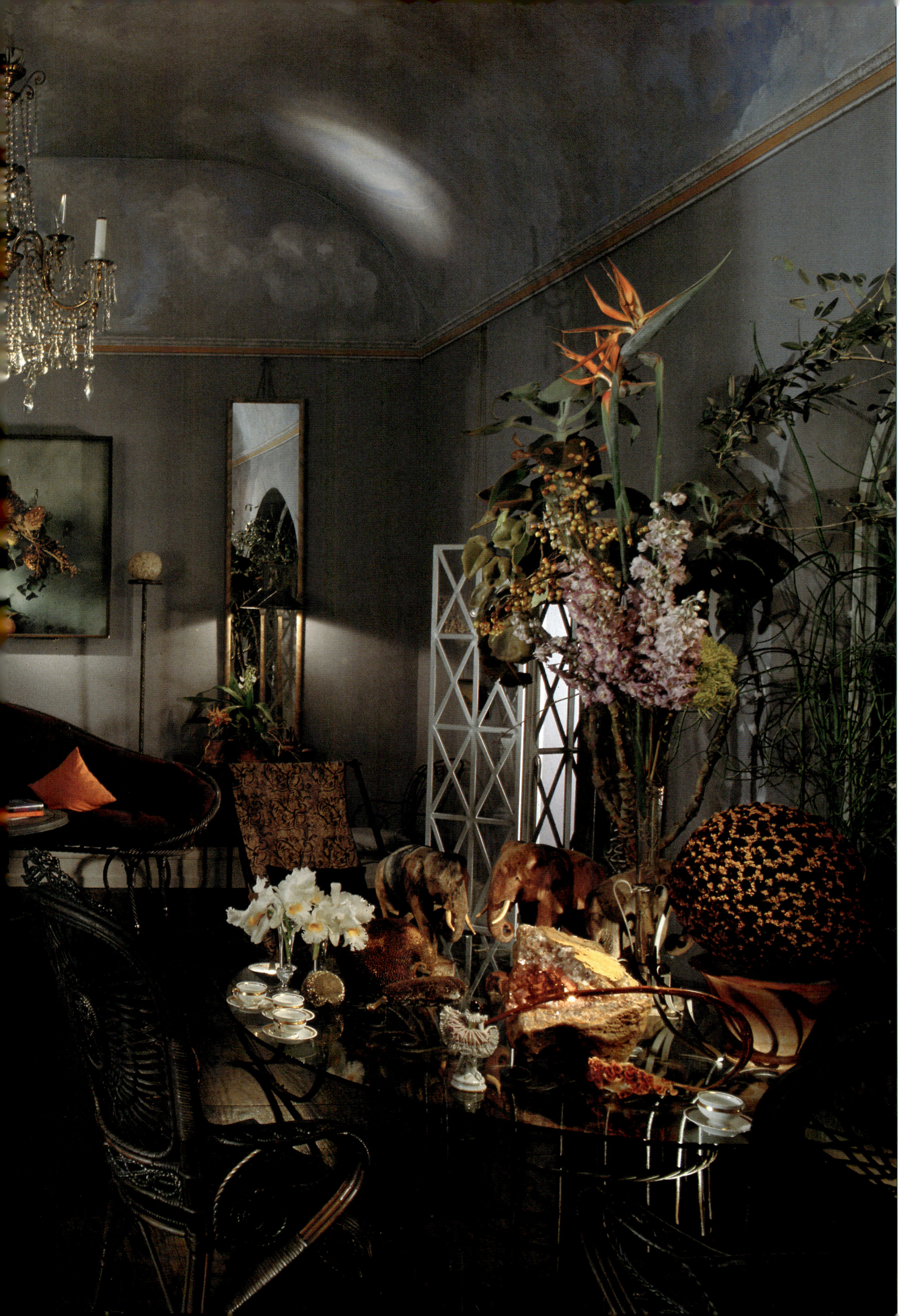

The previously mentioned chaise-longue from the Herman Bang performance (page 198) ended in this setting. The perspective frame on the wall is described on page 126.

The book-shelf arrangement is solved with stacks of books on pillars. Throughout the house, the curtains, which drag on the floor, are linen lined with silk.

*When the doves of the house are not flying
about, they live in the storm porch by the
exit to the terrace.
The female torso is by Pernille Riis-Reffsgaard.*

*On the shelf, a forest of the lady of the house's own creations.
In an adaptation, it is incredibly important to me that
those living in the house are completely in agreement with
the concept and that they themselves put further life into it.*

The tall table lamps are covered with stachys lanata *leaves and carry shades of oxidized zinc. This lamp has become one of my classics.*

*On these pages are shown details and
views from the living-rooms of the house.
The blue hour with a view over the sea —
marked by the divided curtains where
each side can be pulled up and down
individually.*

*Bottom right, a peep into the dining-room,
which is also shown on the two following pages.*

*The dining-room bears — like the arrangement of the
the rest of the house —
the mark of a great joy in collecting.
Many dissimilar pieces, many styles complement
each other on the floor,
which is like that of a banqueting hall.*

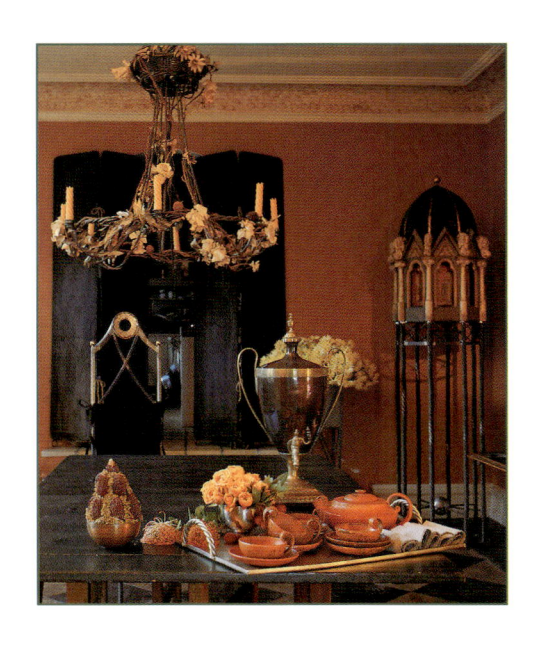

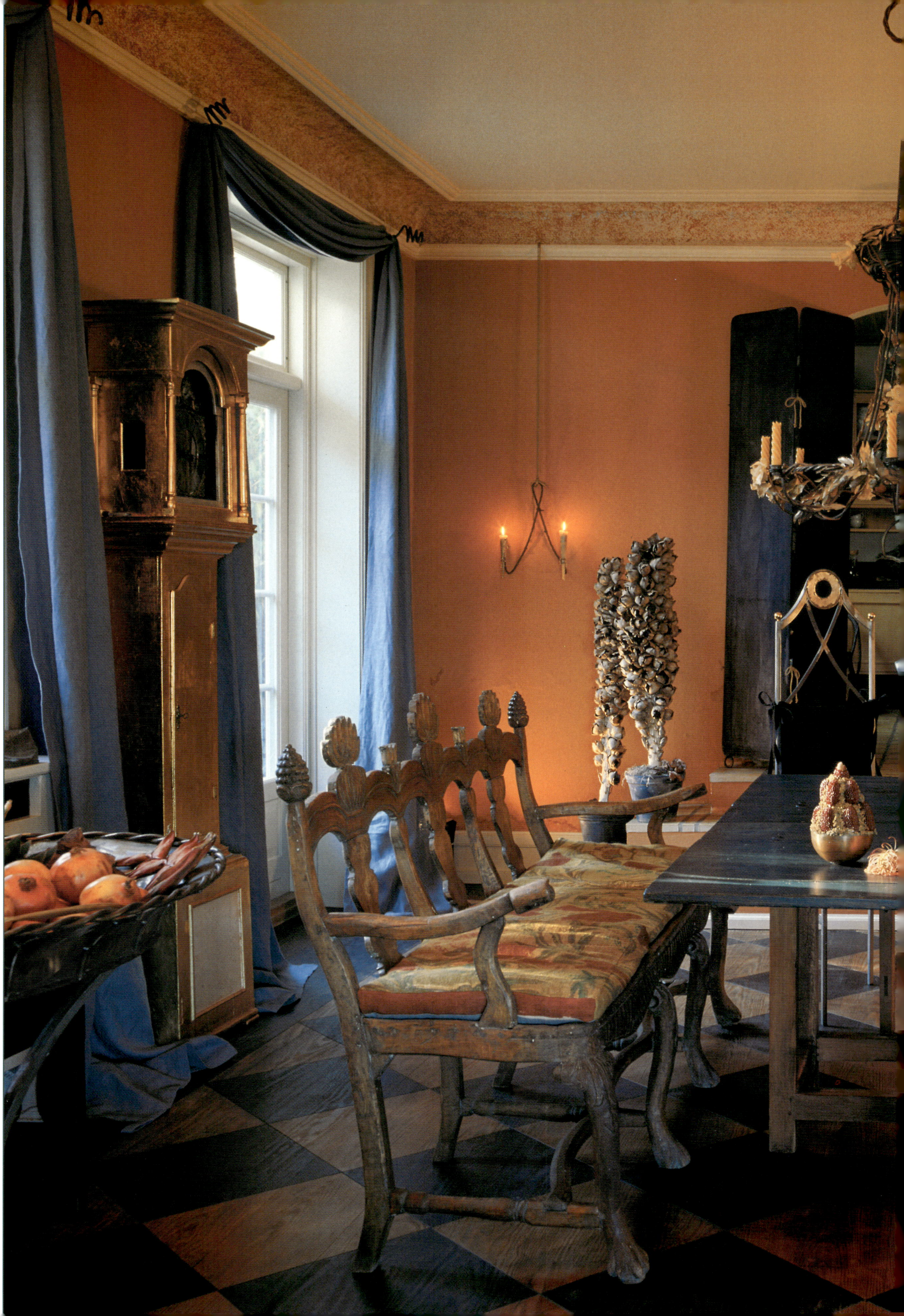

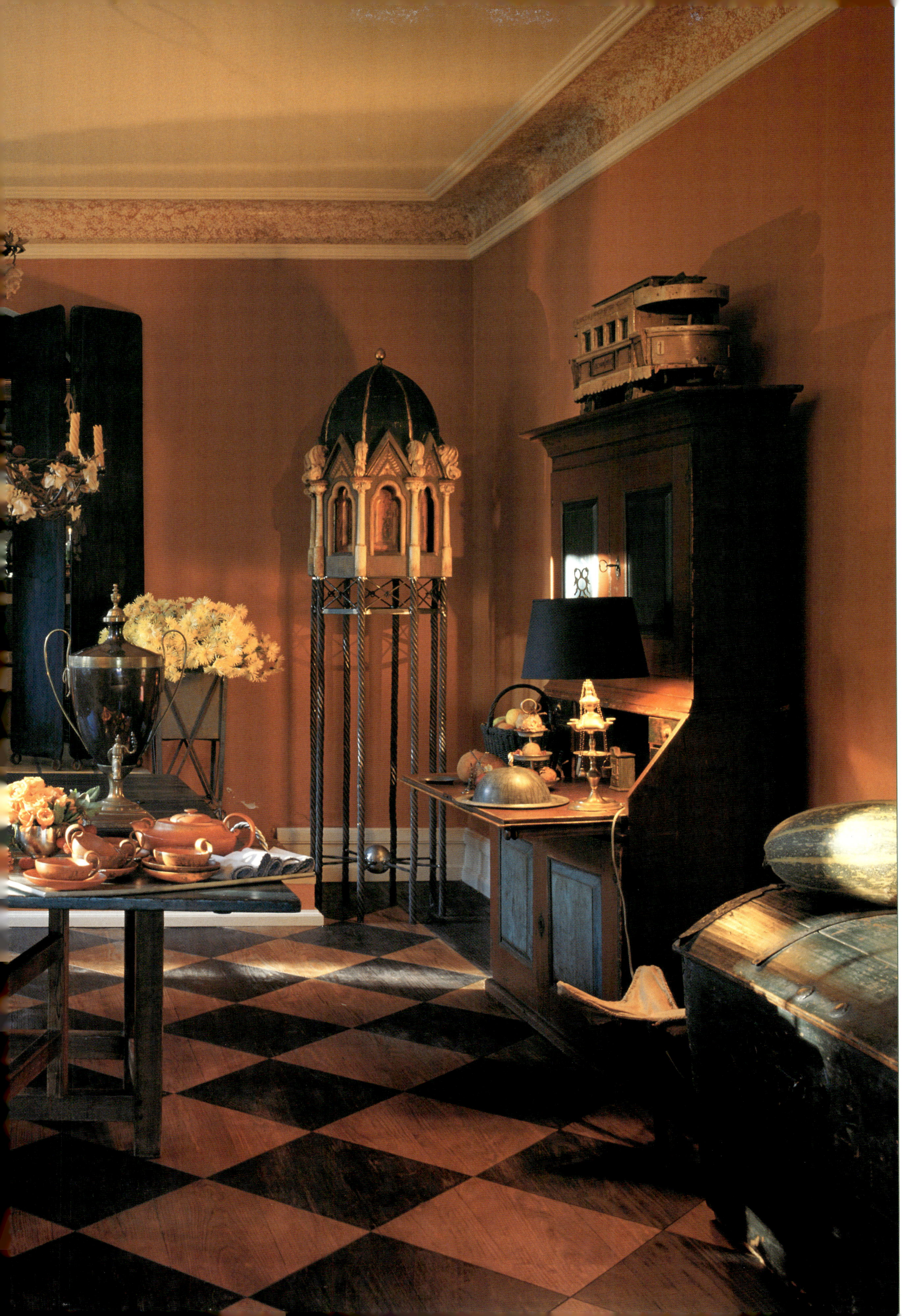

The atmosphere of the dining-room with freely flying doves could have been inspired by the Kremlin.

The bedroom on the first floor has a balcony towards the sun. Birdsong unites with the scent from the euphoriant lilies.

The eye is the mirror of the soul. I like the extremes of existence. Here the balance between romance and the dramatic.

*To finish a decoration is incredibly
dangerous but also almost unthinkable if
the imagination is still followed by . . .*

Let me to compare this house to a cotton coat with a mink lining . . . The neutral exterior and the surprises within . . .

*Christmas or winter chandeliers.
Constructions in iron intertwined with
lichened branches. The pine-cone in the
centre is filled with moss. Concept after
Hans Christian Andersen.*

*Gilded or, as here, silver-plated apples
have long been a tradition in my
Christmases. Gradually as time passes,
the apples change shape until finally, in
the course of spring, they dry right out.
This can also be interesting . . .*

In this, the Christmas of 1990, Christmas tree as door decoration. The bow is clipped from zinc and silver-plated.

Christmas packages await on the stairs.

Hanging candelabras in a row.
The silver-plated stars are
detachable and can be swapped
for other decorations.

The vase basket discussed on p. 189,
here decorated with winter roses and
wreathed pine-cones. The roses are still
alive, covered with lacquer and tinsel,
a quite effective table decoration.

These pavilions were intended as a kind of play-house for adults. The decorations are detachable so that one can change the setting according to one's fantasy. The material is painted zinc, about 80 cm. high.

Silver-plated egg in stand, mentioned on p. 191. The candle snuffer has probably been one of my greatest successes.

Vase basket with red cabbage and stars. Here I feel that I have been successful in making something incredibly simple with a powerful radiance.

Lavender sheaf with birds, here in a haute couture-like version. The draped wreaths and ribbons are easily detachable so that the Christmassy strain can be changed. The birds are cast in plaster.

*Candlestick with shade of pleated silk.
Also called Obsconsole, idea from Søren
Kierkegaard's writing desk.*

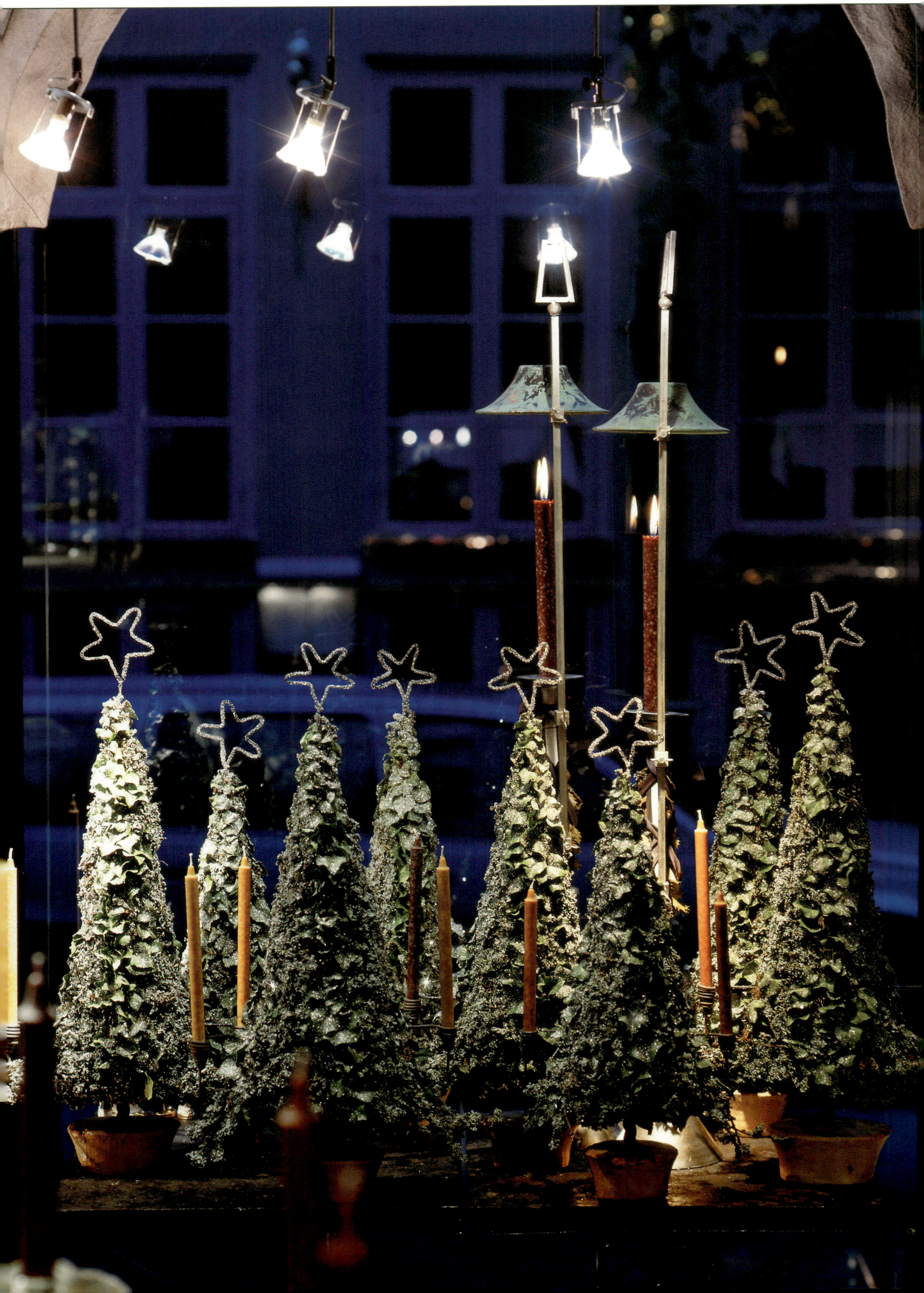

My Christmas tree rich in tradition, which came into being for the first time in 1977 and is now my most requested Christmas decoration. This year, a combination of ivy and lichen.

Right: Scabiosa seed-heads in geometric shapes. Each side has its own effect, so that the bouquet can be turned according to the season.
Below: one of this year's inventions (1990). Twelfth Night candlestick, silver-plated pomegranates on sticks.

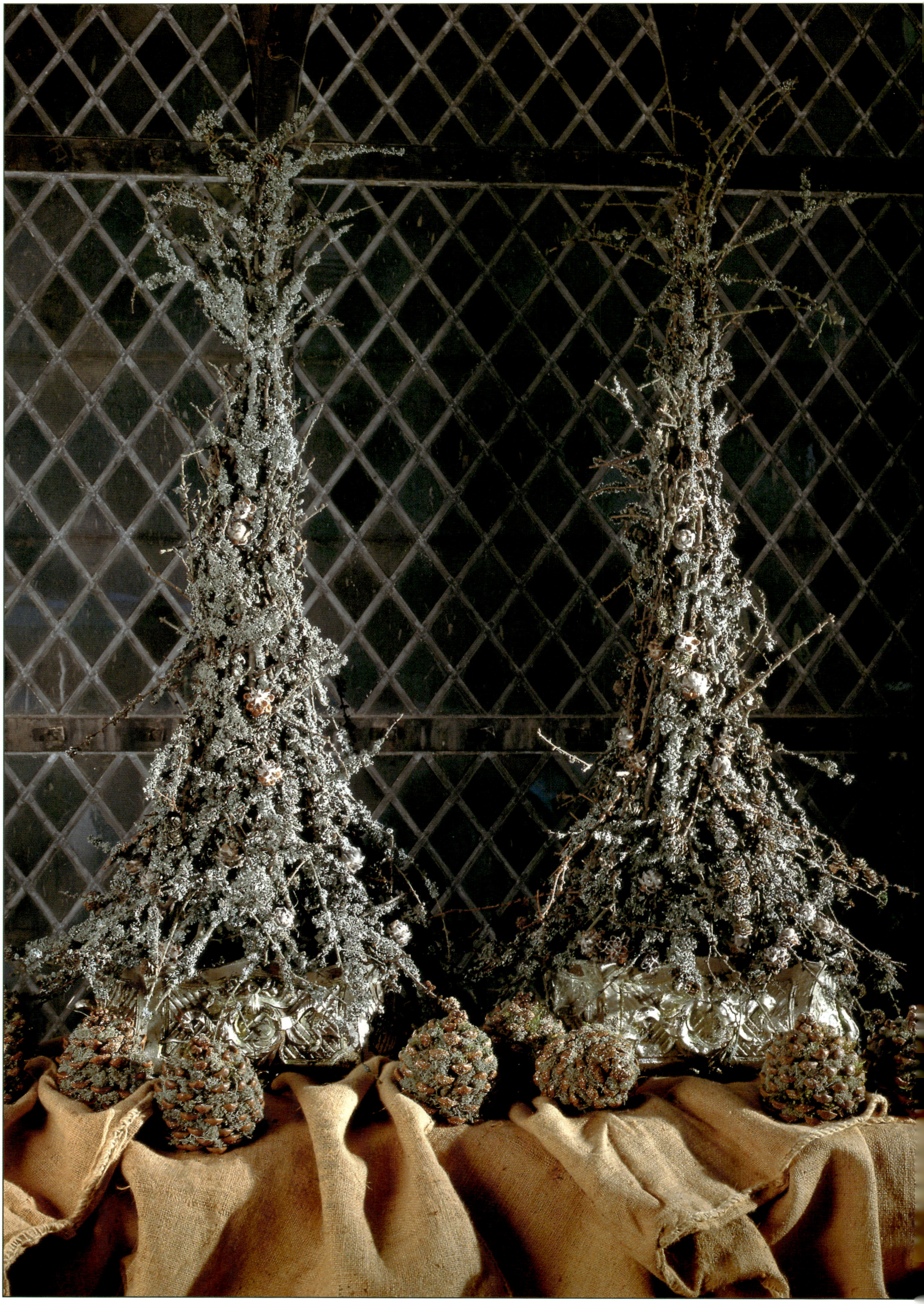

Cover of holly leaves, dedicated to Falsled Kro (Inn) on the island of Funen.

These worthy lambs are made of papier-maché, cast in old chocolate moulds.

Silver-plated iron vases with lichen lining. Part of the Christmas decoration for Restaurant Petri-Pumpa in Lund, Sweden.

*Conch cutlery by Arje Griegst with
assorted personal glass.*

With the Fairy Tale as table companion . . .
Christmas 1990.

A selection of dummy desserts, made for Restaurant Nouvelle (Exhibition Royal Copenhagen 1990).

Bottom: Spun-sugar roses attached to Christmas tree from the previous year (detail from previous page).

Commission: dummy dessert or dessert cover, here containing marzipan tops with crushed nougat, covered with milk chocolate. With it the best brandy and mocca coffee, of course...

In this picture, a kind of grand finale, I pose in the midst of my menage in the honour of my good friend, the portraitpainter Jeppe Eisner. In the summer of 1991.